Influencing Human Behavior

How to Influence People, Persuade Human Behavior and Manipulate Anyone with Behavioral Psychology, NLP and Negotiation Skills

Jason Miller

Jason Miller

COPYRIGHT © 2019 BY JASON MILLER

All rights reserved. No part of this book may be reproduced or used in any manner without the written permission of the copyright owner except for the use of quotations in a book review.

Illustrations Copyright © 2019 by Ralph Williams

Cover photography by Ralph Williams

First Edition: December 2019

Printed in the United States of America

TABLE OF CONTENTS

PART I - THE ART OF MANIPULATION

INTRODUCTION 7

WHAT THIS BOOK HAS TO OFFER? 10

CHAPTER 1: MANIPULATION 15

- Manipulation in a Relationship 15
- What Is Covert Emotional Manipulation? 17
- In-Depth Different Manipulation Techniques 17
- How Do You Deal With Emotional Manipulation? 20
- How to Spot a Manipulator 22
- Early Warning Signs of Psychological and Emotional Manipulation 24
- How to Handle Manipulation 26

CHAPTER 2: DARK NLP – PERSUASION 29

- Seeking Truth 29
- Making a Good First Impression 31
- Building Rapport 33
- Persuading With Emotion and Pain 39
- What Motivates People? 41
- Earning the Right to Ask a Question 42
- Answering Questions With Questions 42
- Softening Statements 43

CHAPTER 3: HOW TO INFLUENCE PEOPLE 48

- Brainwashing 48
- Influence People 50
- Reciprocity 55
- The Pre-Giving Technique 58
- Consistency 67

CHAPTER 4: INTRODUCTION TO SOCIAL VALIDATION, LIKING AND SCARCITY 70

- The "Social Proof" Technique 72
- Liking 74
- Introduction to Authority's Influence 76

INTRODUCTION TO SCARCITY 80

CHAPTER 5: HOW TO TALK 84

WORDS TO USE 84
WORDS NOT TO USE 86
PROBING QUESTIONS 87
ZEIGARNIK EFFECT 88
PATTERN INTERRUPT 90
YES LADDER 91
HYPNOTIC LANGUAGE PATTERNS & EMBEDDED COMMANDS 94

CONCLUSION 100

PART I - THE ART OF SMALL TALK

INTRODUCTION 104

CHAPTER ONE: WHY IS IT HARD FOR YOU TO TALK TO PEOPLE? 107

WHY IS IT SCARY TO TALK TO PEOPLE? 107
WHERE DOES FEAR COME FROM? 109
MENTAL BARRIERS TO TALKING TO PEOPLE 111

CHAPTER TWO: THE FOUNDATION OF SOCIAL ANXIETY AND LEARNING TO COPE 114

HOW TO OVERCOME SOCIAL ANXIETY 114
ADVANTAGES OF LEARNING TECHNIQUES AND EDUCATION ON SOCIAL SKILLS 117
THE CASE FOR LEARNING ABOUT CONFIDENCE AND SOCIAL SKILLS TOGETHER 118

CHAPTER THREE: BUILDING CONFIDENCE FOR BETTER SOCIAL INTERACTION 120

WHERE DOES CONFIDENCE COME FROM? 120
THE BASIC FOUNDATION FOR GROWING THE CONFIDENCE YOU NEED 122
ASSERTING YOUR CONFIDENCE IN SOCIAL SITUATIONS 124

CHAPTER FOUR: UNDERSTANDING THE MECHANICS OF HUMAN INTERACTION 126

THE BASIC PSYCHOLOGICAL PRINCIPLES OF HUMAN INTERACTION 126
DIFFERENCE IN MANIPULATION VS INFLUENCE BASED ON TRUE CONNECTION, INTIMACY AND SERVING OTHERS 128
BASIC IDEAS OF WHAT PEOPLE THINK IN A CONVERSATION AND SOCIAL INTERACTIONS 130

CHAPTER FIVE: THE ART OF SMALL TALK 133

The Goal of Small Talk in Conversations 133
Conversation Flow 135
5 Principles For Success In Conversations 141

CHAPTER SIX: HOW TO INITIATE NON-VERBAL COMMUNICATION 145

How to Smile 145
How to use your eyes/body language 147
How to Come Across and Credible and Confident Without Words 150

CHAPTER SEVEN: BECOMING A MASTER AT SMALL TALK 154

How to Start Small Talk 155
How To use the FORD Method For Small Talk 158
How to Ask Excellent Questions 159
The Power of Listening 161

CHAPTER EIGHT: CHANNELING POSITIVITY INTO YOUR CONVERSATION TO KEEP IT GOING 163

How to Talk and Banter 164
How to Always have something interesting to Say 166
How to Resuscitate a Dying Conversation 168
Step one: Don't take it too personally 169
How to Come Across as a Positive Person 171
Avoiding Excessive Negativity in Your Social Interactions 174

CHAPTER NINE: USING THE ART OF STORYTELLING TO DRIVE CONVERSATIONS 179

Principles of a Good Storyteller 180
How to Keep the Other Person Engaged and Listening 181

CHAPTER TEN: BUILDING QUALITY RELATIONSHIPS AND THE KEYS TO MAKING THEM LAST 184

Connecting with People by Finding Common Ground 185
How Listening Can Help You See and Make Connections 189
How to make them feel like your family 191
The Difference Between Sincere and Fake 193
Timing a Sincere Compliment and How to Insert it into the Flow of the Conversation 195
The art of the compliment (without sucking up to the other person) 196

CHAPTER ELEVEN: SOCIAL INTERACTIONS IN A GROUP SETTING **198**
    GROUP CONVERSATION FLOW 198
    HOW TO JOIN AN EXISTING GROUP CONVERSATION 200
    GROUP CONVERSATION GUIDELINES AND PRINCIPLES FOR STANDING OUT AND MAKING A
    CONNECTION 201

CONCLUSION **204**

REFERENCES **206**

ABOUT THE AUTHOR **208**

PART-I

The Art Of Manipulation

Master the Art of Manipulating and Influencing Human Behavior with Persuasion, NLP, and Dark Psychology

By

Jason Miller

Introduction

When I was at school, I always wanted to be a public speaker. I didn't know that how difficult it was to be one or how challenging it can be to maintain the reputation of being a public speaker. Still, I went on with the venture and trained to speak in the public. I started with college functions and then went on to take part in debate competitions. I loved the feeling that the hall full of people was attentive to what I was saying to them. It was an amazing experience.

I often wondered how some people wielded magical influence over the rest of the lot. How a bunch of people managed to stay at the top all the time. I idealized the personalities of Martin Luther King and other revolutionaries who enjoyed massive public appeal. When they spoke, people listened to them. What they said to them, they remembered it. What they asked them to do, they abided by. Martin Luther King is no more but still his speech keeps ringing in my ears. I feel inspired and influenced. I want to make it happen what he said in the speech. I want to follow him. Just look at the power of the influence he had exercised and still exercises over the masses.

Incredible is the only word we can give it. These people were inspirations. They used to be massive crowd pullers. The thought crossed my mind more than once how could they manage to make people act on their words? Their power over the masses was just unbelievable. What methods they used? What were the words they chose to speak when they were making calls of action? How they used to dress? What were the books they liked to read? What was their talking style and what gestures were common to them when they talked to a single person and what gestures they made when they used to address a massive crowd? All these questions made a chain and kept spinning in my head while I grew older. In this book, I have taken the liberty to answer all those questions. I want you to know what techniques you can adopt to make yourself a highly influential person. How you can make people to like you? How can you be their leader?

What This Book Has to Offer?

This book carries methods and techniques to make yourself a highly influential person. You can read it, integrate the techniques into your personality and exercise a magnetic influence over the masses. Let's breakdown the chapters of the book and see what they have got for you.

- The first chapter of the book revolves around the topic of manipulation. It carries details on manipulation in a relationship and also the existence of covert emotional manipulation in intimate relations. You will get to learn an in-depth analysis of different manipulation techniques that are used by people. Some of the top techniques are devaluation, gaslighting, lying, projections, targeting victims and playing the victim card. When you move on into the depths of the chapter, you will get to know how you can deal with emotional manipulators. Then you will learn about the techniques to spot a manipulator in your friend circle and in intimate relationships. The chapter also carries details on the early warning signs of psychological manipulation. The chapter ends in telling you how you can handle manipulation like a pro.

- The second chapter of the book focuses on persuasion. You will learn the importance of a good first impression that includes being punctual, being original and also the importance of small talk. The chapter also carries details on how to build your rapport with people. How you can communicate in a better way and how you will be able to set expectations. You will learn how you can be able to persuade people with the help of emotions and pain. Other topics in the chapter include the elements behind motivation of human beings. The chapter ends up in explaining how you can answer questions with the help of questions to ease out the pressure accumulated on your nerves, and also certain softening statements that you can learn to make a perfect impression the people around you. The chapter contains the perfect recipe for being able to persuade the people around you.

- The third chapter spans around the methods that can help you learn how to influence people. This chapter is one of the most important chapters of the book. On the back of the knowledge that you have gained in the first two chapters, this chapter goes on to explain different techniques such as brainwashing technique, the features that matter in influencing others, the principle of reciprocity, the pre-giving technique, the foot-in-the-door technique, low-balling offer, the that's not all technique, and the foot-in-the-door technique. In the end of the chapter, you will get to learn about the principal of consistency.

• The fourth chapter of the book focuses on the importance of social validation in our lives. It explains the importance of social validation, social proof and the principal of liking. Then it goes on to explain the importance of the influence of authority. How authority can be obtained and how it can be exercised to fulfill our obligations and achieve our goals. At the end of the chapter you will find a detailed debate on the topic of scarcity. You will learn how you can be able to play the technique of scarcity and shape people's minds and opinion. Some common techniques include the Limited Number technique, the Deadline technique and the high demand technique.

• The fifth chapter, which also is the last chapter of the book, explains in-depth the methods for how to talk to people to leave a considerable influence over them. You will be able to know what words you should use in order to make an impact. You will also get to know what words you will need to avoid so that the listener may not get annoyed and form a bad opinion of you. Next comes the importance of probing questions and a detailed analysis of the Zeigarnik Effect. The chapter contains an in-depth analysis of the yes ladder. You will get to know how you will be able to create a ladder by which you will be able to secure yeses from the customer before getting his agreement on the thing you want them to agree. In the example, I have explained how to do that step by step. The chapter also contains certain hypnotic language patterns that people use to leave an impact on the other person. It discusses the importance of hypnotic pacing statements. Then it explains the importance of subtle hypnotic language. After that it explains how to master the art of hypnotic language. The chapter concludes with the topics of the real value and existence of reality and body language that you can use to increase the scope of your influence over people.

This book carries the right recipe to learn how to influence a large number of people. You should take inspiration from the examples in the book and use them to create your own examples. This book doesn't demand that you should have prior knowledge of the subject. You can start right from zero and then go on to learn to be the master of influencing people. Go on and explore the topics in the book. Have a happy read!

Jason Miller

Chapter 1: Manipulation

Manipulation is a technique using which a person can indirectly control the behavior, emotions as well as relationships with other people. There are lots of people who get engaged in periodic manipulation. When we tell an acquaintance that we feel fine but in fact we are depressed, it is a form of manipulation because we are on our way to controlling the perceptions of our acquaintances and also their reactions. Manipulation has a deep connection with emotional abuse, especially in intimate relations. The word manipulation is perceived as negative when it tends to harm our emotional, physical and mental health of a person.

Manipulation in a Relationship

Manipulation tends to be highly detrimental for friendly and intimate relationships. If it continues for a while, it leads to poor mental health and in some cases, to the death of a relationship. As far as marriage is concerned, manipulation may lead one partner to feel bullied and worthless. It is a fact that bad relationships have the problem of manipulation, but healthy relationships also give room to manipulation, especially when one partner intentionally manipulate the other to ease out a tense situation, kill the chances of confrontation, and attempt to lift undue burden from the shoulders of the other partner. In many cases, people willingly downplay the element of manipulation to save the relationship. In a relationship, manipulation takes a number of forms such as giving gifts, affection, showing a sense of guilt, exaggeration and passive aggression.

When parents try to manipulate their kids, they may make them feel guilty for one thing or another. Excessive manipulation leads kids to depression, eating disorder, and anxiety or some other mental health issues. A study shows that manipulation in a relationship begets further manipulation. If parents are manipulators, their kids are likely to nurture manipulative behavior. Some signs of manipulation in a parent-kid relationship are absence of accountability, overlooking achievements made by the kids and excessive interference in the life of kids.

In a manipulative relationship, the manipulated partner may attempt to meet up the needs of the other partner at the cost of the needs of his friends or family. Guilt as well as excessive coercion are the means by which a person attempts to secure favors such as a job, a loan or any other material benefit.

What Is Covert Emotional Manipulation?

Covert manipulation happens when a person, hungry for power, decides to have control over you by using deceptive methods to make you change your mind, amend your behavior as well as perceptions. Emotional manipulation takes place under the cover of your conscious awareness and has the power to make you mentally captive. Victims of emotional manipulation cannot sort out what is happening with them because it is just so covert.

A person who is skillful in emotional manipulation, makes you hand over your emotional well-being into his hands. Once you do that, he will feed on your self-esteem until you are devastated.

In-Depth Different Manipulation Techniques

If you say that you are clean of manipulating others, you are telling a white lie. We have to use manipulation at one or the other point in our lives. It can be a lie to ease out a certain situation or just a few sentences of flattery to get a job done. Let's take a look at some common techniques that are used by manipulators.

Lying

Manipulators have one habit in common and that is to lie to other people. They use this weapon to wrong-foot people and to confuse them. Lying is mostly used by psychopaths. Sometimes they opt to keep a certain part of the story hidden in order to put the victim at a disadvantage.

Devaluation

Manipulators deploy the technique of love bombing. They will make you realize that this is going to be the best relationship ever. When you are fully convinced that they truly love you, they will suddenly leave you without any explanation.

Playing the Victim Card

Manipulators often take up the role of a victim for gaining sympathy and compassion from the people who are around them. That's how they can attract you because human beings, by nature, try to get close to the people who are suffering.

They Will Target the Victim

When a manipulator stands exposed in front of people, he tries to accuse the victim to cover up his own wrongdoings.

By targeting the victim, he will be able to hide his manipulation.

Gaslighting

Gaslighting is a common technique for manipulating other people. Manipulators ask a variety of questions such as 'You are crazy to say so,' and 'It is in your imagination.' It is perhaps the most insidious technique that sucks at your confidence and the power to feel justified. There are some ways to avoid it and defeat it by grounding yourself in reality and by jotting down things as they had happened. Also, you can open up and discuss it with a close friend. One of the top choices is to contact a support group who can help you recover from this disastrous situation.

Projections

Sometimes manipulators want to blame you for all the bad things that are happening to them. Everyone does that once in a while but psychopaths make it a routine business. Psychologists say that this is a kind of mechanism on the part of psychopaths who want to extricate themselves from the guilt of possessing negative behavior by linking them to someone else's behavior. If you detect anything similar in the behavior of someone close to you, don't shower any compassion on that person. Instead keep a strategic distance from them. (Stillman, n.d)

How Do You Deal With Emotional Manipulation?

There are lots of people around us who are always fabricating a plot to manipulate others by making them feel ashamed of themselves or by snatching their happiness from them if they don't follow their injunctions. Emotional manipulation is quite hurtful for people. Let's see some of the brilliant ways to deal with this problem.

Don't Open up Your Heart in Front of an Emotional Manipulation

People sometimes say, 'I am quite sad to hear that you would think that I forgot your wedding anniversary.' These words make us feel guilty even when we have done nothing to hurt others. There is nothing left to say or apologize to them. You don't have to feel guilty and you should not say anything to those people. The key is not to take care of what they are saying or doing. When you are dealing with an emotional manipulator, you should trust your gut and senses. Manipulators are always looking for a hint and once they find that weak spot, they keep hitting that.

In the above example, you asked the manipulator if he had forgotten your wedding anniversary or remember it? In response to that, they made quite a dramatic scene by putting the guilt on your shoulders for just asking this question.

Emotional Manipulator Is a Always Willing to Help

Some emotional manipulators are always looking for something they can agree to. When you ask them for help, they will take deep sighs to show as if what you are asking them to do doesn't suit them. When you ask them that it doesn't seem like they want to do what you are asking them to, they will turn the tables on you, saying how unreasonable you are for thinking so. If he agrees to do that, hold them accountable for what they do and how they do that. Don't further delve into the details. If you feel that they don't like to do that, ask them to stop. If this is not possible, go take a hot shower or a stroll on a lonely pavement, covered in autumn leaves. Enjoy what nature has to offer. (Harmer, n.d)

Emotional Manipulators Tend to Fight in a Nasty Way

Emotional manipulators like to keep things really nasty. They won't hesitate to backbite you, and also coerce and manipulate others to tell you what they wouldn't have said otherwise. One of the easiest things to note about them is that they won't show active aggression. Instead, they will be highly passive in demonstration of anger. Also, they will create pathways to let you know how unhappy they are with you. For example, they will convince you that they will support for your new job yet when you join and have to consume lots of time on office work such as creating power point presentations and charts or graphs, and get busy as a beaver in the work, they will play loud music in the home or watch TV late at night. If you dare ask them about the reason for this behavior, they will go on with their excuses and say you just cannot expect life to stop. They can be so much annoying to say the least that at times, you will want to strangle them that will land you in jail.

How to Spot a Manipulator

It feels like hell to be emotionally manipulated. Emotional manipulation is considered as highly destructive, which is why it is vital that you know how to recognize a manipulator in your life. The feat is not as easy as you might think because manipulators are skilful in what they doing. Gradually, as they see positive results, they will keep raising the stakes over time. They will be doing their job and you won't even realize what is happening. If you know the signs of an emotional manipulator, you can easily detect them around you.

They Will Play With Your Grasp of Reality

Emotional manipulators are skilled individuals when it comes to crafting lies. They will make you realize that something didn't happen when in reality it had happened. They attempt to influence our sense of reality. They are so good at doing that they we end up questioning our own selves whether what they are saying is right. In fact, we start doubting our own sense of reality that ultimately causes confusion. If you spot someone attempting to change your perception of reality, you should insist that it all sits in their imagination, and that it has nothing to do with reality. Don't let it overcome your senses.

They Will Play the Victim Card

Emotional manipulators can be easily detected because of the fact that they attempt to play the victim card more often. Whatever is becoming wrong in their life, they try to blame it on someone else. One or the other person finds himself in hot water when manipulators get caught up in an incident, because they start complaining that they have been wronged. They think that if they are unable to do a job, it is someone else's fault for setting high expectations.

They Will Not Hesitate to Hit at Your Weak Spots

Emotional manipulators always know about your weak spots and they won't stay back to push them when they get an opportunity to do that. For example, if you are worried about losing your hair, they will pass a comment on it in front of strangers or the girl you want to marry. If you are insecure about your color, they will not hold back on discussing the same in front of everyone. If you have to prepare a project to present at the office, they will try to discourage you and intimidate you by pointing out how the participants will judge you and question you. That's how they can shake your confidence and make you feel bad about the other day.

Early Warning Signs of Psychological and Emotional Manipulation

Psychological manipulation is done through mental distortion as well as emotional manipulation in order to seize power and gain privileges at the expense of the mental peace of the victim. Here are some tricks that manipulative people keep up their sleeves for coercing others and push them into a disadvantageous position. There is a difference between habits and manipulation, but it is you who must be able to recognize it.

When someone is trying to manipulate you, he will try to make you speak first. He will try to ask you inquisitive questions that would establish a baseline about how you think or behave. This helps them evaluate your strengths as well as weaknesses. If someone is asking too much questions that you find properly crafted and planned first, you are being targeted as the speaker might have a hidden agenda for doing that. This kind of psychological manipulation can happen in an intimate relationship or at the workplace with a colleague. The best course to take is to listen to them, check their behavior, and answer well-thought replies until you are able to tell if the person is doing that intentionally or by habit.

People also try to manipulate you by intellectual bullying as well. Some people consume considerable time on collecting facts and figures about a number of things in order to be an expert. Also, they want to be more knowledgeable in different areas. In fact, they want to show everyone that they are the experts in a certain field or more than one field. Not bad if they have studied hard and authentic facts, but the problem is that they advocate alleged statistics and facts, and also incorporate other data in their speech that is alien to you. They attempt to download from their brain such information that you don't have access to. If they are doing that for educating you, you will know from gestures and expressions. Manipulators hope that they are able to impose their agendas on you. By exhibiting themselves as experts, they will use this technique for no other reason than to make you feel inferior, unsettle you, and then use you for their personal benefits.

People at the helm of affairs in the government sector and the corporate sector love to entangle people into a web of paperwork and red tape. They use their position to manipulate others into submitting to something they dislike. Bureaucrats also use their influence to delay any kind of fact finding into their wrongdoings in the office.

How to Handle Manipulation

Manipulators can be your parents, intimate partners or even kids. There is no solid definition of a manipulator which makes it hard to handle. You can tell that you are being manipulated if you are losing power in a relationship, and also when conflicts are replete with emotional factors.

The first principle to deal with a manipulative person is to feel safe in a relationship. If you are not feeling safe anymore, you ought to develop a plan for maintenance of your health. You need to find a person whom you can trust and who is there to listen to your explanations. If an intimate relationship is failing in making you safe, you should remove yourself from that environment temporarily or even permanently if things don't appear to be coming back on track. Tell your intimate partner or a family member that you will not tolerate their screams and that you will not come back to their home until they stop shouting at you. Try out the following things:

1. Lock your door to cut off communication.

2. Get yourself out of the apartment.

3. Stop the car if you are driving and he is shouting at you unendingly.

4. Refuse to accompany that person in the car.

5. Pack up and leave the apartment to live in a hotel or with a friend.

You should wait for the right time to talk if you must initiate a conversation with the person who is manipulating you. When you think that the boundaries have been crossed, you should freeze for a moment to decide on the limits once again. You may choose not to escalate a tiny argument into a big one.

When your partner feels rejected, it is not the right time to initiate a conversation. If you are ready to confront the manipulator but you also know that the person is vulnerable to your threats such as leaving the apartment, you should wait for the right time to initiate the discussion. Confront them when they are in the state of listening. Then expose them. If the manipulator happens to be one of your parent, you should walk cautiously. Don't do anything in haste. Usually parents are not expecting this kind of behavior from their kids that's why you have to keep the tone of voice moderate. Especially if they aged, they won't be able to sustain any aggression. Speak with reasoning.

Another top tactic to handle manipulators is to take a non-combative approach for fighting back whenever you get attacked. You cannot take out anything productive by arguing so give your partner time to speak. Listen to them in a calm state and try to absorb what they are saying, and then react to it in a sensible and calculated manner. It is not easy to state your point of view when the other person is making exaggerations or exhibiting emotional intensity. Amidst all this remember one thing that you can always say a big 'No' to something you don't approve of.

Chapter 2: Dark NLP – Persuasion

The basic idea behind the development and study of Dark NLP is that people don't have any concrete identity and they have a lot of characters to take up. Dark NLP means that the fluidity of identity of a person offers a gateway for manipulators. This fluidity pushes them to adopt a personality that manipulators are looking for. They start behaving as per the will of others. This pushes them into a circle of malicious influence by manipulators who use their dark spells on them.

Seeking Truth

Stoicism has a few central teachings such as it reminds us about how unpredictable our world can be and how short time span our life has. How we can be strong and how we can take control of ourselves are the questions that everyone needs answers to. It deals with perhaps the greatest problem of our life that is the absence of logic. We usually get carried away with the flow of our impulsive behavior that entertains our senses rather than logical reasoning.

Stoicism is different from the other schools of thought in that it is practical and is not concerned with just our intellectual faculties. To succeed in the world, we must be able to do things that we would not have done in normal situations. Most of us don't try to do things that they should be doing in order to succeed in life perhaps due to the fear of unknown.

Most people trust things as they are appearing to their eyes without realizing the fact that the reality can be way more different. We should be seeing things in our surrounding as they would be, had we not been there. Our surroundings demand that we focus on what feel they are giving off such as how they are looking. The effect the sun light or the artificial light has on those surroundings can be a subject to study. You should closely observe the movement, the animals and the landscape of the place you are in. Notice the soundscape of the area.

When you are able to keep your focus on this, you will observe that a unique sense of simplicity will arise out of it. Things will appear to be more poignant. Try to disconnect from your surroundings to see the real form of things. Most people have formed a habit of looking at their surroundings through the lens of how it is going to affect them. This affects our judgment of things. We try to form a connection of things to our lives to assess whether they will fit in or not in our lives. For example, a luxury car belonging to a person will make you realize that you don't own one. When a person is taking off a holiday, it will make you realize that you don't have a holiday.

That's a self-centered and self-referential lens. You should better avoid that to see the truth behind things.

The problem behind why we don't see the truth is that we don't want to see things as they are. Short glimpses of things as they are, are always there for you. All you need is to disentangle yourself from your own self and then see things as they ought to be. In simple words, we should be objective when observing our surroundings. Subjectivity colors our judgment and we can only see things in relation to how they are affecting us and not how they, in reality, are.

When we adopt this attitude, we are able to see things in a broader perspective. Every scene we will see will carry a unique signature and a unique identity to express. Even a parking lot has a unique identity to offer if you don't see it as a space for your car to stay for a while. This practice can be applied to the people around you. Notice them as if they don't have any connection with you and you will see their true self.

Making a Good First Impression

When we meet someone, it takes a few seconds to judge his personality and evaluate him. You will form an opinion of him and the other person is also doing the same during the time of your meeting. We forget the latter part most of the time. He will take notice of the dress that you are wearing, your gestures, your mannerisms, and also the way you have done your hair. Each day we meet new people who try to evaluate us and form impressions of our personalities. There is a common saying that the first impression is the last impression. It is a truth because once a person has concluded the process of calculating the first impression of your personality, he is unlikely to alter it or reverse it. Without a doubt the first impression sets the tone for the relationship. Thankfully, we can learn some smart techniques to create a brilliant first impression.

Be Punctual

You are on your way to inking a business deal and you have to meet your business partner for the first time in a hotel. If you make an excuse that you are going to be half an hour late, the other person is not going to be interested in your excuse for getting late. Even if he waits for you and finally signs a deal, he will have it in his heart that you are not a reliable person. Schedule your time as such to reach a few minutes earlier than expected. You should keep in mind the possible delays such as a traffic jam, and work on it to cut down on delays and be on time for the meeting. (Making a Great First Impression, n.d)

Be Original

Making a good first impression means that you ought to blend in with the other person for a while. It doesn't mean to lose yourself or pretend to adopt a fake personality. The best possible way to make a lasting impression is to be yourself in front of the person you are meeting for the first time. In this way you will not have to wear a fake persona each time you meet him. You will feel more confident, build solid trust and also earn respect as well as integrity from your partners.

Small Talk

If you don't open communication with the other person, it is impossible to create an impression. What topic you choose for small talk, what tone you are using, what words you select to express your thoughts matter a lot when it comes to starting a conversation. Take a couple of minutes to learn about the person. Talk more about his interests and likings. Try to know him. (Making a Great First Impression, n.d)

Building Rapport

Rapport is generally a two-way connection between different people and it must stay so. It is not something you can create yourself. In fact, you can learn how to stimulate it by following some simple steps. The very first thing to look after when you are trying to build a rapport is to give a check to your own appearance. It will help you form a connection with people. It must create a barrier. You can choose a dress that is slightly better than the dress that the other people are wearing. You should go for a modern dressing arrangement. If you think that you have excessive dress layers, remove some clothes to suit the situation. You won't want to be the butt of all the jokes cracked in a party.

Some Basics to Take Into Consideration

When you are communicating with someone, you should keep in mind the following basic elements.

- You need to express yourself as culturally appropriate. Criticizing a particular culture or talking too much about cultural taboos will present your persona as a culturally inappropriate person that is not good for business and other social matters as well.

- You should wear a smile on your face when you are communicating with the other person.

- One important thing to keep in mind is to remember the other person's name when you are communicating with him. It helps you build up a more personalized approach toward them. This brings us to

Dale Carnegie's best seller book 'How to win friends and influence people.' Carbine argues that the key to win the hearts of the other people is to remember their names and then addressing them by the name when you meet them in future.

- When you are talking to someone, you should hold your head in an upright position and also maintain a good and confident posture.

- The key to building a good rapport is listening carefully to what others are saying to you. You should be attentive to the minutest of the details they are trying to discuss with you.

- The most amazing thing is not to overstay your welcome at any place you go. Don't let others get fed up with your presence.

Elements of Communication

There are three different elements of communication to make a killer first impression. Let's analyze them.

Mirroring: The first of all in Natural Language Processing technique is mirroring. This suggests that a person's behavior should match that of the others so that there should be no barrier in the communication. When the other person doesn't remain comfortable in talking to us because our behavior is making him reluctant, a communication gap is a must to build up. Mirroring helps us overcome such barriers.

Controlling the flow of conversation: This is yet another important element in conversation. We have to learn to control the flow of our conversation. It is not anything such as dictating other people or simply overpowering them in the conversation. The main objective is to fully engage the listener into what you are talking about. It doesn't mean that you start being coercive in the communication, but instead you should be able to engage the other person into the idea that you are trying to download from your brain.

Setting expectations: Once I met a client to ink a business deal. We had a good chat in the half-an-hour meeting that we had. The next day I texted her to inquire about a missing point in the proposal and to know whether she wanted me to include it and email her the updated proposal. I expected her to respond in ten minutes but she didn't reply until I sent a second text around eight hours later. During those eight hours I kept thinking if that person liked me or not or if she was considering my proposal or not. I had set wrong expectations and this kept me on the edge. We should set expectations to the minimum and as natural and logical as we can whenever we see a new person. This is minimize undue pressure on our nerves.

How to Set Expectations

This section contains a short step by step guide on exactly how you can set expectations in any conversation. The very first step is to understand that it is very hard to set and then fulfill expectations. You should be able to verbally articulate or write on a piece of paper about the expectations you have for the other person. The next step is to know when you should set expectations such as the time during the conversation when you need that. How to communicate or when to communicate them?

You need to help people see the bigger picture. They should know the 'why' factor behind the expectations that you are trying to set. When they understand the reason behind setting expectations, they are likely to fulfill them. For example, you are expecting them to finish a job in a thirty minutes timespan. You should tell them why it is important to finish the job in a short window of time. Once they know the 'why' factor, you have successfully set the right expectations.

When you are done with the initial steps of setting expectations, you should move on to have a couple of meetings with the other person to discuss about the expectations that you have set to know whether they are on schedule or not and also how they are approaching the said project.

You should be regularly conversing with whom you have set your expectations. They may have expectations from you. The ideal scenario is that both of you get your expectations fulfilled. Better for business and long-term commitment.

It is always a good idea to bring your expectations into written form as written things offer us greater clarity. Unwritten things are dependent on our memory that's why chances are high that we may forget them.

The last step is to get agreement from the other person that he will fulfill his expectations. Also, give your agreement to the other person that you will fulfill all the expectations that the other person has set for you. This kind of mutual understanding will boost up confidence in your relationship.

Expectations can be set and fulfilled by mutual agreement. Usually, we fail in communicating what we expect from others in a lucid way. This ambiguity takes its toll on our relationship. When the ambiguity is completely removed, the next step is to stay committed to what you have agreed upon. This builds up the base for a long-term relationship. Good for business!

Persuading With Emotion and Pain

The most prevalent behavior among people is that decisions should be based on logic. We love to be rational because we think this kind of behavior will help us succeed in life, but we forget along the way how much power emotional persuasion has. There are particular emotions that help in persuasion. On top of all of them is sadness. It is a kind of emotional pain that is characterized by the feelings of loss, helplessness, sorrow and disadvantage. Sadness slows down the pace of decision-making. It creates a fog in your brain and compels you to make decisions that are viable only for a short-term. In addition, sad people are spontaneously drawn toward happiness. If you have the ability to appeal to their sadness, you can persuade them and influence their decisions.

Anger is another emotion that you can use to persuade people. It can be defined as an intense emotional response. It suggests that the basic boundaries of a person have been violated. Latest studies suggest that angry people are more capable of analyzing things and also distinguish between weak and powerful arguments. In the moment of anger, you are more in control of things, experts believe. If the amount of stress is reasonable, it will give a major boost to your optimism.

If you take a look at different marketing campaigns, you will know how business strategists are using these emotions to persuade people into buying their products. When you appeal to a person's emotions, you are on your way to creating a lasting connection with them that brings them in the perfect state to respond to your calls to action. When the connection has been established, they can understand what you are trying to convey to them, and they will accept it as well.

You should understand how it is working on you. Analyze a couple of businesses and charities and see what emotions they stir up inside you. Think of the ad of a company that provides controlling services for roach infestation in houses. Think about the picture of a roach getting killed by an employee from the pest control company. What emotions does this billboard stir up in you? It should be a combination of anger, anxiety and happiness. You get angry and anxious because you recall how much destruction these roaches have brought to your home, but finally you become happy that the pest control company is going to get rid of it. This will compel you to follow their call to action. You are easily persuaded when the marketing campaign played with your emotions.

What Motivates People?

Active listening is a skill that you can acquire and also develop with untiring practice, but most of the time it is a difficult skill to master as it takes considerable patience and time. Active listening means that you should fully concentrate on what is being said to you instead of just hearing what the speaker is saying. It involves use of all your senses. You can show the speaker that you are an active listener with the help of verbal as well as non-verbal messages. The most common gestures are eye contact, smiling, nodding and saying yes or no in order to encourage them to continue. There are different gestures and signs that show that a person is actively listening to what is being said.

Smile: some people express their tendency to actively listen to the speaker by passing slight smiles off and on. You can pair up your smile with the nod of your head to make them more meaningful.

Eye contact: if you are looking to the sides, the speaker will take it as a non-attentive gesture. Eye contact is a must to show the speaker that you are actively listening to him. However, in some cases, eye contact can be intimidating for a shy speaker. You have to determine how much eye contact you need to make an impact. For leaving a healthy influence, you should add a couple of smiles to the eye contact.

Posture: your posture tells a great deal of details about your personality and habits. Attentive listeners develop the habit of leaning forward while they are listening. Active listeners also tend to give a slant to their heads.

Earning the Right to Ask a Question

Have you ever wondered how a salesman sell products to a big number of people? He carries solutions to the problems of people. Selling is not about convincing people into purchasing a product. Instead, it is about tracking down what people want and then providing them with the same. It is about helping people manage their lives in a better way. When an entrepreneur is producing a product, he has to keep certain questions in his brain. He has to ask the right questions from himself. If you don't ask the right questions, you don't know what the needs of the buyers are and how you can fulfill them.

Answering Questions With Questions

If we talk in general, people don't like a question in response to a question as an answer. But doing that has significant advantages. Perhaps one of the best feelings is that it relieves the pressure off your back and diverts it to the one who is asking the question in the first place. It helps because as long as you have to answer questions, you will be on the defensive side and you will have to feel the discomfort attached to answering questions. By throwing a question in response of a question, you will push others into the same situation in which they gave pushed you earlier on. Some questions are less a question and more an attack on the listener to unsettle him. This method is the best to take the heat off of you and channelized to the speaker. This method will also help you set the tone and the temperature of the conversation you are having with the other person. If you are answering a question with a question in response, you are on your way to get an answer that you would otherwise not have achieved. This is how you can get yourself out of stick situations by answer tough questions with questions.

Softening Statements

This section highlights how to soften your harsh statements or questions using a simple technique. One day I rushed to a bank to pay my bills as I had to take a flight to Los Angeles where my daughter and wife waited for my arrival. We had planned a vacation together. The line at the billing counter was a pretty long one. I broke the line and approach the cashier while a woman, who had been there for quite some time, stood there and saw what I was doing to her. She waited for a full minute before shouting at me and asking me what I was doing. "What do you think you are doing young man?" she almost shrieked into my ears. I took a glance around me to see who she was and why she was shouting at me. It was then that I realize that I had broken the line. When I heard the shout, I got mad and I really wanted to do the same to her, but I held back and asked the cashier to help her first. This really calmed her down and her anger vanished into thin air in a matter of seconds. She was an old woman. I realized that I would be in her place someday. Yelling is normal to many households. I grew up in the house of yellers. My parents and siblings loved to do that and it was not always done in anger. Yelling refers to the tone of our voice, but a sharp sound appears to be really harsh and brash. I got used to it as I spent around twenty years listening to this.

I had married to a calm and peaceful girl who would loved to convey her messages in a polite tone. Kirstin was a beautiful lady who would calm me down whenever I happened to burst out in anger. She advised me to lower down my voice tone whenever I was in anger. She believed that a calmer tone really helps in settling down a hyper situation. That day in the bank I remembered her instructions. I handled the situation by responding in a polite manner to yelling and anger, and consequently it helped me defuse a charged situation, saving me from unwanted embarrassment. I was happy for myself because I was able to deal with situations in a calm manner.

All this happened because I transformed harsh statements into soft statements and it worked pretty well. If you want to skilfully handle charged situations, you should be able to soften somewhat harsh words and tune them to normal. For this purpose, you will have to bring some changes to your personality. The first is to admit that your approach was wrong. I admitted to the lady that I had done wrong by breaking the line, and I should not have done that. The admission of doing wrong melts the hearts of people who even have a heart like a rock. The second and the final change is to submit to accountability. In my case, I was accountable to my wife whom I had empowered to snub me and chastise me whenever I got off the right track. (Mobley, 2014)

Let's take a look at some common examples of softening harsh statements into soft ones. Often, companies use the word downsizing instead of laying off when they are wrapping up their man power. In this way loss of jobs doesn't sound negative. This technique is known as euphemism in English literature. English novelists were fond of using this technique.

Finance companies nowadays use the following words when they are revealing their forecast for the next few months. Their director may say that they had reduced the forecast for the second quarter, but the word 'reduce' sounds negative and it will leave a negative effect on the stock market. Instead, they say that they had adjusted the forecast for the second quarter.

Instead of saying that the company has decided to cut salaries by 2%, they would say that the company has decided to cut down costs or control expenditures. These kinds of softening statements help business improve their image. Better for their business! Softening statements are like a magic spell as they calm down hyper sentiments and anger and project a positive image of an individual and a company.

They are often used in the stock market business. Investors and traders use the word 'negative sentiments' when the stock market nosedives. Apart from that when a particular stock is lagging behind the others, they say that the stock is going through corrections after a rally instead of saying that the stocking is shedding value or is coming down the hill. If you take a look around certain business campaigns and news, you will get to know that business across the word vigorously follow this technique.

Chapter 3: How to Influence People

The world is a complex place to live in and survive. Only the fittest can survive and nowadays being fit means being able to wield a massive influence over people so that people are ready to listen to you and forgive your wrongdoings. If you are a manufacturer, you cannot sell a product unless you learn the trick to influence people and change their minds.

In this chapter I will explain how you can be able to influence people and what its benefits are. You will learn about a number of methods that can be used to shape the opinion of others in your favor.

Brainwashing

Brainwashing is often referred to as a thought reforming and a well-planned technique to influence a person's behavior, beliefs and political opinion. The term has its origin in the United States, surfacing in the military circles when a big number of American military prisoners defected to the communists after getting captured by the Korean military. The soldiers were returned to the United States but the military high-ups were alarmed to learn that the American soldiers were not thinking and acting the same way as they had been trained. A few of them had been harboring anti-America doctrines and had been appreciating the Marx methods to rule over a nation. It all happened during their incarceration period. Experts found out later on that the soldiers were subjected to sleep deprivation and psychological manipulation that are broke down their personality and autonomy.

Nowadays, the United States and other countries who are at war against terrorism believe that the same tactics are applied on the people that are used by religious organizations. We call these people extremists and terrorists. This helps us understand why a sixteen years old teenage girl, who has so much to see and do in life, jumps into a crowd of people and blows herself to pieces in a terrorist attack.

Brainwashing is considered as an invasive form of influence and it demands full isolation which is why it is possible in prisons and in terrorist camps that are mostly isolated from civilized society. It is crucial for the agent to exercise complete control over the target in order to conclude the brainwashing session in a conclusive manner. By complete control, I mean the control over his sleeping patterns, eating schedule, washroom and bathroom needs and any other basic human need such as the need for some fresh air. Once the agent successfully wipes out the data on the brain of the target, he replaces it with a set of beliefs, behaviors of which the target had previously no knowledge.

Some psychologists say that brainwashing is possible under the right conditions while others consider it as a milder form of influence than the media considers it to be. Some definitions of brainwashing demand that the presence of a threat of physical harm is imminent in the brainwashing session while others say that there is a type of brainwashing that don't rely on nonphysical coercion as a means of influence. Experts do believe that the effects of brainwashing to influence others stay for a short span of time. They believe that the popular belief that the target loses his unique identity when he embraces the new planted identity is not right as his true identity is not completely lost but is pushed down into hiding inside the brain. Once the agent stops reinforcing the new identity, the target will recover his old behavior and beliefs. So the verdict is that the agent must reinforce the new identity of the target in a regular manner. (Layton, n.d)

Influence People

You have influence power so do everybody else has. It is the ability to motivate as well as inspire the masses to take action. The power of influence is what makes you stand out among the rest of the lot. This is the major difference between a leader and a manager. Influence, in general, refers to one's ability to exert a positive effect on others in order to convince others to gain support. When you are able to exert influence on other people, you get the power to persuade them and engage them toward an idea.

It is the application of power for gaining the results that you want or to achieve certain objectives for yourself or for an organization. Experts believe that people try to use some key techniques such as logical reasoning, socializing, exchanging, consulting, building alliances and modeling. At the same time there are some dark sides of influencing others such as intimidating, avoiding, manipulating and threatening.

Experts also believe that influence is not an easy feat to pull off. We exercise influence over our kids, partners, and friends and at a bigger level, countries exercise influence power over other nations. The power to influence others is always inside us. All we need is to unleash its potential and reap its benefits. It is a fact that we need a little bit of polishing. Whenever we attempt to affect how most people think and behave or make a decision, we are exercising our power to influence them. Similarly, a smile and even a simple handshake help us socialize with people and influence their opinion. Whenever we break down barriers with strangers, we get into a position to influence them. If you want to know whether people are getting influenced by you or not, you should see if they like you and your thoughts. If they do, they have already been influenced by you. All you need is to kick off the process and get it going. Gradually, you will realize that they wouldn't be able to say 'no' to your requests.

The top rational approach to influencing people is logical persuasion of other people. You should use logic to explain what you need to believe and what you want others to believe. People sometimes are greatly attracted toward logical persuasion. You should tell them what you think about a particular business or an idea. When you communicate with them, they get a chance to your opinion and your thought process. That's how they are likely to appreciate your thoughts, and when they do that, you have got the power to influence them. They will listen to what you say and very possibly do what you want them to do.

Socialization is another tool that is brilliant when it comes to influencing others. By socializing with different people, we get a chance to be open as well as friendly with them. We can talk about their achievements and appreciate them. We can also appreciate their thoughts and opinions that allows us to bring them into our friend circle. The trick is a simple one. We should keep in mind that every person on the planet loves to hear his reasonable praise that's why when we are appreciating someone for a reason, we get great influence over them, which we can use later on.

Another popular technique that we normally use is asking questions from people when we are trying to initiate a project or launching a scheme for our business. Engaging others into giving their input is a brilliant way to bring them into your magical circle of influence. People love when you give them importance and request them to leave their input for your projects. They like to express their opinion on the pros and cons of a particular scheme and how it will affect your business. If you ask them to pass a review on your business project, they will appreciate you and form a positive image of you in their brains. That's where your power to influence them starts. They will listen to whatever you say.

The power to influence can be lethal in the hands of manipulators. Manipulators also use some common but dark techniques to negatively influence others. They will force others to act against their best interests. To accomplish this objective, they will avoid their responsibility and put it on the shoulders of other people. They can use deceit and lies to attain their objective. Also, they will be seen disguising their intentions and withholding certain information.

Manipulators also try to impose themselves on other people by forcing them to comply by using loud voice, arrogance, abrasion and insensitivity that is a preferred technique for bullies. The most heinous technique they can use is to threaten other people to harm them in case they are unable to comply. The threats can be the show of weapons or by describing an example of someone who had been subjected to their wrath for non-compliance of their orders. This is the technique that despots and dictators have been rigorously using throughout the history of the world.

The Features That Matter in Strengthening Your Ability to Influence Others

Leaders have a unique ability to influence others. They master the skills that are needed to assume the role of a leader. These abilities include learning agility, the power of communication and self-awareness etc. If you cannot influence others, you cannot make reality what you have envisioned for the world or for those who are around you such as your family and friends. The people who want to lead don't just command over others but they also become inspiration for others. They know the art of persuading others and also encouraging others. They tend to tap the knowledge of a particular group and direct certain individuals toward some lofty goal.

Leaders should build up a politically savvy mindset. They should also build up a special skillset to view politics at a neutral level and as a crucial part of an organization. They must understand how important politics is for the health of an organization. They should do proper networking to develop their social capital that must include a special mingling strategy. Leaders should think before they respond to people, and also set goals before you decide how to express yourself. In addition, leaders should pay close attention to active listening.

Another important feature of the personality of leaders is that they maintain a robust foundation of trust among employees or followers. Leaders should learn to trust first and then demand the same from their followers or employees in an organization. That's how they are able to convince people to comply with what they say and what they demand. Trust is vital for the growth of an organization, and it helps deal with the toughest of challenges in a fruitful way.

Reciprocity

Let's start this section by understanding the principle of reciprocity. I'll go over the norms of reciprocity and how they can be utilized for powerful influence. I'll show you how to think about applying reciprocity to your own attempts to influence people.

The principle of reciprocity is the basic of foundation of a relationship. It can be defined as one of the most crucial human needs to give back something they have received from the other end of the relationship. When I was a kid, my friend gifted me an expensive fountain pen on my fifteenth birthday, a couple of days before the party. I wasn't used to receiving expensive gifts from friends in that way, but I was really happy because nothing in the list of my birthday gifts even came close to its lush and glamor. It was simply brilliant. The friend was so selfless that he even didn't show up at the birthday party so that I might not remain under his influence because of the gift he had given to me. The birthday cake was cut and the night had gone, but I couldn't forget that pen. I had a powerful urge to return something to him before I started using the pen, and I did exactly that. I didn't use that pen until I gifted him an equally expensive wrist watch. It is human nature that whenever we receive something from person who doesn't had given it without expecting anything in return, the urge in us to return the favor gets the strongest.

If you take a closer look at the world around you, the world is full of reciprocities. When someone takes a favor from his colleague, he returns it with a thank you. The communication doesn't stop there. The person who receives it, returns the favor with a welcome, and it happens on a daily basis. Our brain is naturally wired to return something in exchange for what we receive. Just imagine a girl who has been receiving gifts from her girlfriend for one year but has not reciprocated the favors. Will they friendship last till the end of the world? It is hardly likely that it will. Only the relationships that are built on the principles of reciprocity tend to last for a while. Also, they last until the principle of reciprocity is violated. The same principle works between a buyer and a seller.

You can integrate the principle of reciprocity into your personality and it will help you maintain a healthy and powerful influence over other people. The best strategy is to give something to others without expecting anything in return from them such as a discount and a bonus. If you are businessman and sell a product, you will be able to double up your customer base by using this method. You can offer some gift or some other incentive such as a 'buy one get one free' thing on your product. Also, in return of the package or the favor, ask the customers to leave an email or a message on social media in praise of the products or services of your company. You can offer them access to emails, social media groups or any other forum where they can easily leave their feedback.

You can also thank your customer in reciprocity when you have sent the order. You should take up a personalized approach for thanking your customers. Address them by their name and be specific about the product or service they have requested. Then go on to thanking them from the core of your hearts. That's how you can build a positive image of your brand and also make yourself highly influential.

The Pre-Giving Technique

Pre-giving is the most basic reciprocity technique, and it involves a very simple way of gaining influence. The basic idea at work behind this technique is that when you give someone a physical gift, you will be able to secure favors from them in return. Your likelihood of exercising healthy influence on them increases. Even if the gift you are giving someone is a small one, you are basically creating an expectation that the other person will reciprocate it and that too with gratitude, just because you have made the first move. That's why pre-giving becomes highly important in terms of exercising influence over other people. It shapes up or positively contributes to our first impression on the other person.

A study was conducted to look into the technique of pre-giving and also judge how effective and beneficial it is. Participants believed that the person with whom they were interacting was just another participant while in reality he was one of the actors that researchers had hired to conduct the study. They were only pretending to be participants. In the middle of the experiment, the actors requested the other participants leave the place for a couple of minutes. When they got back, the experiment continued normally as it was getting on before. Sometimes the actor didn't return empty handed, but he had a pair of Coca Cola bottles in his hand. On entering the room, the actor told the real participant that he had brought the drink for him. So the participant received a gift from the actor just like we exchange gifts in normal days.

When the experiment ended and the two participants, one of them an actor, were packing up to leave the room, the actor told the participant that he had been selling raffle tickets and that if he sold more tickets, he would win a prize. It was like a competition so the actor asked the participant if he would buy any tickets. The researchers wanted to check the reaction of the participants.

When the results were prepared and unfolded for the public, it turned out that usually a person is willing to buy just one ticket, but the participants of the study were willing to buy two tickets on average. That was an amazing turn of events. They agreed to pay double price just because they had received a gift in the form of soda from the actor. This showed when someone gives a gift no matter how humble it is in terms of value, we are highly likely to follow his directions. This is a spontaneous reaction which sometimes we cannot explain. Reciprocity principle immediately gets into action when the person demands something from us.

There are certain elements that are crucial for the functioning of the pre-giving technique. It must be kept in mind the time span between these two things should not be extraordinary long. The shorter the time span is, the higher will the compliance level from the other person. The study showed that after the week had passed, the results were slightly different, but a month, the results had totally changed. The effect of the gift and the influence it had brought to the giver had gone into thin air. There wasn't much effect on the participant.

We can give an absolutely free gift just like the one that actors in the above mentioned experiment did. It can be a physical and a free gift. It can be in the form of free content that you offer to your customers in the form of blog posts or eBooks or email letters. When you are providing them useful information for free, you are actually making them feel indebted to you. Another method is to send wish cards to your customers to special occasions such as Christmas or New Year. All the things have the sole objective to give away something absolutely free to your customers or the people around you. The pre-giving technique turns out to be pretty much helpful in business. The key is to give away a gift then ask them for a favor in a short window of time. The favor should be a reasonable one and something that the customers can easily do. (Reciprocity technique #1: pre-giving, n.d)

An Overview of Common Persuasion Techniques

Persuasion can turn out to be a Herculean task if you don't do it right or you don't tread the right path. Convincing a single person on your viewpoint is pretty tough. Just imagine convincing a dozen or a group of fifty people. Still, there are lots of people around us who are pretty expert at convincing others, and they always leave us wondering why it happens that some people have a better ability. Have you ever met a salesman of any company? Some of them are pretty good at cracking a deal with a customer. Convincing others is their bread and butter. They have that steel confidence in their personality that they will be able to convince the people they met to sell things. Psychologists have successfully crafted certain techniques which you can use to boost up your convincing power. Let's review those techniques.

The That's Not All Technique

Although an influence tactic in the "reciprocity" family yet the That's Not All technique takes a different approach to utilizing this principle. Marketers use this technique for persuading potential customers who are still thinking about what to buy from the market. This is a special technique because of the fact that it takes into account making a request and afterwards putting great emphasis on the benefits of the product or service with the help of additional arguments before you ask the person to comply with your request. For example, your salesman is selling motorbikes at a showroom. The hall has been filled with around one hundred customers who are here to buy motorbikes. The showroom has five other companies that have put their products on display. All of them have salesperson who are actively working to sell maximum items. Your salesperson tells the customers about the benefits of buying the motorbike such as great speed, economical average with respect to consumption of oil and lots of other benefits. There is one rider who is demonstrating how the motorbike runs and how it sounds. Just before your salesman makes the call to action, he adds, "That's not all. When you buy the motorbike, you will get ten liters of gas as bonus." (Common Strategies: Common Persuasion Techniques, n.d)

Ten liters of gas is just peanuts in front of a bike that is worth several thousand dollars but the impact it makes on the minds of buyers is huge. It is a free gift from you for them. It will add great strength to your persuasive arguments.

Foot-in-the-Door Technique

The foot-in-the-door technique is a genius application of consistency norms to maximize the chances that someone will agree to do something for you. It's not as violent as it sounds--I promise! This technique involves making a little request that a person is likely to agree upon. When he agrees on the little request, you can go on to make a larger request. You can understand this by the name of the technique. When you are able to step a foot in the door, you are ready to walk through the other doors. When the buyer agrees to your first request, you can secure the right to make them agree to the second favor. Sales personnel use this technique to boost up sales. For example, the salesman for your motor bikes may ask a random customer, "Do you mind telling me which company's motorbikes you ride?" (Common Strategies: Common Persuasion Techniques, n.d)

The customer will think that he is doing a favor to the salesperson by just telling him the name of the company. He will be interested in the question thinking that the workers are doing a kind of survey to collect data about the people who are bike riders. Bike riders usually love to answer questions about their bikes. Once the first question gets an answer, the salesman can go on to ask the next question.

"Why don't you try our bikes? They are a good ride as compared to your current bike?"

Starting a conversation in this way helps you secure more clients than directly asking them to buy your product or switch to your service. A number of studies have supported this technique as the best technique for salespersons to sell different products. First make a small request and then deciding upon the response of the customer, go on to ask for a bigger favor. This strategy can be applied to any household item such as soap products, electronic devices etc.

Door-In-The-Face Technique

In one last instance of reciprocity in action, the "door-in-the-face" technique takes yet another perspective on how to take advantage of reciprocity norms. This technique is just another method to make a request that tends to operate in the back way. Using this technique, you can make an unreasonable request that the other person is going to refuse right away. This method is quite beneficial in sales negotiations. For example, a motorbike salesman, may offer a customer to trade his old bike for a new one from your company by offering the customer a tiny amount for his old bike. We know the result of this request. The customer is going to refuse it anyway as it was intended by your salesman. When he has received the refusal from the customer, he will then turn toward the customer once again and come back with another offer that is more reasonable than the last one, and that he thinks the customer will incline towards. Even if the second offer is going to be lower than what ought to be reasonable, the customer is going to accept it because he has already been subjected to a ridiculously low offer. (Common Strategies: Common Persuasion Techniques, n.d)

Experts explain that one reason behind the influence of the door-in-the-face technique is that it plays on the sense of guilt of the customer. They realize that they had already declined the initial request of the salesman that's why they should accept the second request. The sense of guilt starts getting over their nerves that they have not helped out the salesman upon the first request. When the second request is made and it also appears to be more reasonable than the first, the customer readily agrees to it. The second request offers them an opportunity to decrease the level of guilt that the customer had experienced.

There is another explanation why this technique worked, and that is the refusal of the customer to the first request gives birth to a grave concern on the part of the customer that his reputation has been torn apart. They may feel that the salesman considered them as uncharitable or somewhat rude or even uncooperative. Let me explain this in simple words.

As human beings we are always looking out for a second opportunity whenever we do something wrong. The second request by the salesman turned out to be that second opportunity that the customer had been thinking about. He grabs it and satisfies himself by presenting himself as a fair person. (Common Strategies: Common Persuasion Techniques, n.d)

Low-balling

The low-ball technique is one more way of utilizing the consistency principle to maximize your influence. Using this technique involves being careful about how you present all the necessary information. The low-ball technique is about making a request to the customer and then gaining an agreement on the same from him. You have to change the terms of that deal at the nick of the time. This is an unethical method of securing agreement from the customer, but that's the way to do that.

Take the example of a motorbike salesman who may tell his customer that he is selling a bike for $15,000. The customer happily agrees to pay the price, thinking that he has received the best deal for the bike. Everything is agreed upon. The time comes to sign the agreement papers. It is then that the salesman reveals that the price he told the customer was incorrect, and now he could only sell the motorbike at

$18,000. The customer had been waiting for a long time in your office, during which he has made up his mind to purchase the motorbike. That's why he agrees to buy the motorbike at a higher price. This technique also is about saving your reputation in front of the salesman and the other staff. (Common Strategies: Common Persuasion Techniques, n.d)

Consistency

The principle of consistency can be explained from the fact that people, in general, desire to be consistent in words and deeds. Can you recall an event when you had made commitment to a person but could not fulfill it? Did it make you feel good or was it a terrible experience? Most if the people consider it a bad experience. They think it is embarrassing and shameful to leave a commitment in the middle.

People, usually, are highly likely to do things in which they feel more consistent with. They adopt the attitude that they most of the time carry and feel comfortable with. Consistency is considered as an adaptive behavior that really helps when we are trying to influence others. The world is really a complex web in which only the person, who has made up habit to make decisions and do certain acts on a set pattern following a set of values, can survive.

People feel bad if they say that they will do a thing and then change their mind and say that they cannot do that. This inconsistency is also considered as an emblem of unreliability. We tend to struggle for consistency in the commitments we make. We have to keep up with our values and attitudes when we are faced with acting on some plan of action. We have to keep up with our attitudes that we have trained over the past several years.

It is human tendency to not only be consistent in reality but also be able to portray himself as a consistent person. You can do that by making public what you do. You can also talk about it in your family and friend circles. Share it with your partner and friends in addition to mentioning it in your social networks. It works two ways. When people know about our habit of being consistent, they create a sort of pressure that keeps us moving with the same level of consistency. The second benefit is that it portrays our image as a person who doesn't compromise over his principles. It will definitely add to your power to influence people. When you say something, people will be expecting that you will stand by it and that's why they will listen to you and act on what you say.

Chapter 4: Introduction to Social Validation, Liking and Scarcity

In this chapter, I'll cover the basics of social validation, including its relationship with conformity and the way psychologists have understood its effects. Social validation is the greatest way to motivate people. Let me deal with this concept by explaining what symptoms to watch for when you are seeking social validation. Each of us has to go through a certain time when we are subjected to a unique environment due to one or another reason. Sometimes it is because of our new job in a different than in which we have been living. Sometimes it is because of our studies when we have to live in a different city or country to attend a university.

If you have been subjected to a new environment, the chances are high that you might have observed what people do around you. Whenever you meet a stranger, you try to mimic their gestures and language to blend in the environment. This is our first attempt to seek social validation in a totally new place. We just don't want anyone to stare at us and call us a stranger or check our behavior.

If you look at social validation through the lens of psychology, it means that a person is conforming to a social group and also following actions of that particular group to blend in their company or simply to win their trust. Social validation is about adjusting your gestures, language and appearance in accordance with where you are going to or where you are living in. The phrase, When in Rome, do as the Romans do, can explain how social validation works.

Social validation is all about conforming to the traditions of the current environment that you are living in. Adaptation to an alien setting is a natural process and we unintentionally do it sometimes.

Social validation follows the principle of conformity. When a customer is not sure if he should go ahead and buy something, he has to rely on the reviews that other users have made on the benefits of the product. Only after that they are convinced that they reviews are great, the chances of their making the purchase considerably increase. Social validation works on the principle of liking and conformity by a great number of others customers.

Consumers are more likely to buy a product that their peers endorse to them rather than going for the product that celebrities endorse. Consumers are more likely a buy a product from Amazon if it has a good number of positive views.

The "Social Proof" Technique

This theory was first advocated by Robert Cialdini who maintains that a person who is unaware who to behave in a certain social circle, will look forward to other people. Social proof is something that help us discern what is right from the eyes of the other people. what other thinks correct becomes right in our eyes.

When we cannot judge a situation ourselves, we look out for social proof to validate our judgment. Social proof reinforces our judgment or totally reshapes it as well. Social proof works well during the time of crisis when we don't have sufficient time to think and make a decision. Social proof shapes our behavior and the theory that explores and confirms this notion is known as the Informational Social Influence Theory.

Applying social validation to the compelling influence is pretty straightforward. I'll give you some specific mechanisms of how social proof can be used and why it's so effective.

The first mechanisms is uncertainty. It is the fuel that tends to fire up and also feed the mechanisms of social proof. When we face an unfamiliar situation, we become uncertain about the result of the circumstances, that's why we feel the need to refer to our social circle for guidance on the matter. It is a kind of reassurance that we are doing the right thing.

Another mechanism is similarity that tends to motivate us and also enhance our social proof. When we identify ourselves with a group of people, we are highly likely to attend to their recommendations and suggestions. The similarity can be based on age, color, race, nationality, language, physical appearance or some job occupation. Studies suggest that we are more likely to follow the guidelines laid down by our peers with whom we share a similarity.

Social proof helps us move around our social circles without any fear of rejection or odd behavior on part of our peers. We can protect ourselves from taking actions that would make us feel alienated from the society. When a company sells a toothpaste, it includes a tagline that four out of five doctors have recommended it use. That's how they try to validate that our peers have confirmed the use of a particular toothpaste. Testimonials by someone from our social circle are more likely to click our minds than endorsement by celebrities.

There are some dangers of social proof as well, and they can be quite detrimental and hazardous. For example what our peers are doing is not the right thing. If we follow them blindly, we are going to land ourselves in great trouble. Social proof is considered as the most powerful weapon to persuade and influence people. If we use it in the right way, we can be able to improve our personal lives and social interactions.

Liking

Why do companies hire sexy models to sell cars, energy drinks and perfumes despite the fact that it is the males who are greatly attracted toward sport cars and energy drinks? Liking is important when it comes to exercising influence over people. Customers want a website to look good to convince themselves that it is credible and likable. It should have a brilliant design and unique functions that must offer users enjoyment during the time they have to click all the buttons.

If you take a look at the website of Black Clothing, they are hardly using any high quality photos for the visitors to soothe their eyes. Instead they have uploaded a fun video at the start of the website. Users watch this video and enjoy the introduction before they enter the website and explore its pages. The video features multiple hot and beautiful models who are wearing Black Milk Clothes, and are having fun as the preparations for Christmas go on. Liking can be a powerful influence strategy. I'll further show you exactly what

I mean by "liking" and why it can be such an important tool of influence. The customers who happened to like the video, are more likely to buy the products from the online store. So physical attraction does wonders when we are trying to get people to like something we want them to.

One especially useful tool for increasing your likability and aiding in your influence attempts is the similarity technique. I'll show you a few examples of this technique in action and also show you how to think about applying this strategy yourself.

This is the second principle of liking. Most of the brands that are being produced across the world fail to relate to the customers. We prefer to purchase things from a company that loves to interact with its customers and is quite empathic. When a corporation gets involved in live interaction with people, people start liking it and its products because they try to find a relationship with the company and the product. For example, Ufone, a cellular company, has created a logo Ufamily. The users of the company now boast of being a part of the Ufamily. They have found a relationship to nurture and take care of. They buy its products because the company has offered them a new identity. They like their slogan and that's why they buy their services.

Nowadays big brands are working hard to cut down on the distance that exists between the customer and the company. They have started to realize that they cannot behave like an alien or a superior being who have the responsibility to provide the customers what they cannot produce themselves. They know that they have to be a friend of you to sell their product. You have to build a kind of reliability as well as similarity. When you know that your customers can relate to you, you can better understand their problems that they face and then provide solutions in accordance with it.

Yet another tool based on liking is the familiarity tactic. You'll see a few examples of familiarity in action, and I'll also dispel some myths about what has to occur for someone to benefit from "familiarity." By using this technique, you can make a conscious effort to create familiar face prior to making a request. This strategy results in greater compliance in response to the request that you make. People are highly likely to get influenced by the ones they are more familiar with. How to create a sense of familiarity among the people is a challenge that you have to take up.

Introduction to Authority's Influence

It should come as no surprise that authority figures have huge influence. But why? And how deep does that influence run? Influence largely happens when a person or a specific group tends to affect some other person or a group. Power is the capacity of a person or a group of people to influence other people or groups. On the other hand, authority is an offshoot of power that is given in the hands of a specific individual group.

There are number of people who surround us all the time. Among them are religious leaders, doctors, teachers, police, military men and fire fighters. They are people who are in the positions of authority. They are highly revered by the masses because by nature human beings respect authority and power. When a doctor says that we should be consuming sugar, we refrain from it. When a doctor asks us to take medicine for two weeks, we abide by him because we respect what he says. Similarly, when a cop asks us to get out of the car, we respect what he says because of his authority. When a professor of a university asks us to consult a specific book, we go to the market to buy that because we respect his knowledge.

The point is that we like to rely on people whom we consider as having superior knowledge in a particular area such as a medicine, health, teaching, law or other specialized fields. People across the world get easily swayed by the influence of those who are at the helm of affairs. If you are running a business and a staff of fifty is working under your control, you are an authority figure for them. Leaders and manager must understand the principle of authority as it has turned out to be a powerful tool for exercising influences over people.

Where authority is easy to exercise, it also is easier to abuse. It is important you use it in a measured way so that you can be able to maintain your trust among employees. Once you lose the trust among the people who are under your authority, it is nearly impossible to rebuild the same. When you start exercising authority over the people, the other principles of persuasion become easier to implement. An important thing on authority is that you should not be using it for personal gain. If you do that, you will have to pay for it. You will be held accountable for that. You have to use this principle wisely and you will be happier than ever and will be able to bring about more productivity for your firm. To exercise authority over people, you have to take care of the following principles. Let's talk about them one by one.

The very first principle is of aestheticism. You have to present yourself as the one who is immensely careful of his aestheticism. How you present yourself to others is important when you are an authority figure. It has a deep impact on your staff or employees. You have to be able to look like an authority. For example, you should wear an expensive dress suit with a tie that should have a neat knot. Look like an authority figure if you want to be one.

Also, you should buy an expensive sports car that communicate to the onlookers that you possess a high status. If you cannot buy a super costly car, you should keep your old and cheap car well attended. It should be spotless and well-maintained. Always do your hair and don't forget to pay attention to self-hygiene. In short, they should be inspired by your look, and in this way they will be more ready to follow your lead. That's the way human brains are wired. Another aspect of aesthetics is that they boost up your confidence.

You have to remain engaged to exercise your authority especially on new hires in your organizations and new employees in your company. These new entrants will turn out to be a fresh start for you as a leader. You should personally help them so they can navigate through the company and absorb key information that you want them to. You should make sure that they are getting access to all the information you want them to absorb. Also, help the fresh hires to absorb themselves in the culture of your company. Also, communicate the mission, values and vision of your company to the fresh hires along with the 'why' factor behind those values and the vision. You need to welcome them in a way that shows that you are extremely excited for them to join your company.

Remember that if you want to influence people with your authority, you should walk your talk. People start getting annoyed from a person who fails to walk his talk. You need to lead by example. If you want your employees to work from 9 to 5 without a break, you should show them that it is possible by doing them yourselves. If you don't like your staff to wear jeans at the office, stop wearing them yourself.

Last but not least is that you should highlight the achievements of your employees before the other staff members. We love attention, appreciation and a round of applause. This will encourage other employees to follow in the footsteps of the high achiever. In addition, it will boost up their confidence in you as a leader. They will respect you more than ever for respecting people who work hard. It is like the reciprocity principle in terms of appreciation and respect. (Eisenhauer, n.d)

Introduction to Scarcity

Yet another influence principle is that of scarcity. I'll review the nature of this influence principle and why it does what it does. The persuasive power behind making something scarce or limited to attain is quite powerful.

The "Limited Number" Technique

One application of scarcity that you've probably seen a million times is the limited number technique. I'll review a classic study from the science of influence to discover a few refinements of the basics of limited numbers. Cialdini identified that scarcity are among the top six social influence principles that are used to elicit compliance, choice and agreement. Burger and Caldwell conducted a study to assess the impact of the principle of scarcity. They invited some participants for an experiment by making them believe that their personality test scores had been rare. They told them that they fall into the category of the top ten percent. Other participants were told that their scores were more common. The remaining participants believed that the opportunity was unique and scarce so they were more likely to show up and participate in the exercise to make it to the ten percent. In general, research alludes to creating shorting of something in terms of numbers. Just as we saw that participants came again and again in droves to be a part of a bunch of people. The scarcity of the group madly pulled them. One of the many people to make people think is that the quantity of something is reducing. When people are convinced that the number of slots or items are limited, they will be attracted toward it. (Nicholson, 2018)

High Demand

The second principle is creating a high demand. If they perceive that the demand of something is high, they move toward attaining it. In order to elicit scarcity, you need to make sure that the thing is in high demand. For example, avocado remains in high demand in the sub-continent which makes it more desirable and precious. Now apply the same principle to humans. You should develop certain habits and collect such knowledge that people are always willing to listen to you. You should also invest in yourself in terms of training so that people seek after you to gain something useful for their professional life and tips to solve their work-related issues. A person who has 100,000 followers who are ready to listen to his words is considered as highly influential. That's the reason people who have a following on Twitter, Instagram or YouTube are considered as influential. Remaining in high demand is the key to wield a powerful influence over people.

The "Deadline" Technique

Another scarcity tactic is to employ a deadline. You know this one well--or do you? It turns out that the deadline tactic isn't all it's cracked up to be, and I'll show you when this strategy can actually backfire. You can make a choice scarce by setting a time limit around it. You can put an arbitrary deadline on the option and ask people to go for it. This technique can really backfire because humans don't like restrictions. They love to be free that's why they are more comfortable in open scenarios in which they have free time to ponder over something and make a decision accordingly. If the deadline is too short, most people will fail to act thinking that they are busy and they have been subjected to injustice by being offered a short deadline. If you must set a deadline, you should create a strong call to action and keep repeating it in the ears of your customers so that they pay heed to it. One of the best call to action can be: start acting now before time runs out. (Nicholson, 2018)

Chapter 5: How to Talk

This chapter will show you how you can improve your speech that could make an impact on the masses. You will learn about certain words that you must include in your speech, words that you should do away with and techniques to use hypnotic language. You will also learn how to master hypnotic language and how you can use your body language to increase your circle of influence.

The chapter contains discussions on the Zeigarnik Effect, the Yes ladder, probing questions and pattern interrupt. You will be able to tune your speech to make it more effective and full of power.

Words to Use

Experts say that the biggest problem of the world is that we cannot persuade people to do what we want them to. We always have to confront defiance and most of the time, defiance wins. If we want to influence others and motivate them to do something, we have to convey our message in the right words. This brings us to choosing the right words to communicate our thoughts and desires. It is not just necessary for persuading people for a short while, but this ability to persuade others is also necessary for building up a good leadership quality. It demands certain stellar communication skills and also has the ability to boost up human connection. Let's go through a rundown of some magic words that can do a tremendous job while we are communicating to others.

The first word is 'Yes.' This word is a part of a lot of languages other than English. What is at the top of the fears that lots of people across the world harbor? It is the fear of facing rejection that keeps us. Our brain is wired to link the word 'no' to rejection, and that's what our brain doesn't accept. This means that the word 'yes' has a totally opposite effect on our brain. 'Yes' is perceived by our brain as a positive word and a sign of mutual understanding. If you use this word more often in your communication, you will be able to connect to the positive part of the brains of your listeners. This works perfectly well if you apply this technique on your marketing campaign. Your customer wants to be accepted by you. By hearing a streak of 'yeses,' they will be able to ease out the tension that is accumulated in their brains. Studies suggest that you should incorporate at least three yeses into your speech to make your speech effective.

The second most important word in your speech should be their name. When you call someone by their name, it means you appreciate them and value them in your life. It is the best way to win someone and bring her on your side. A person's name is the sweetest sound he can ever hear.

The most important word among all is the word thanks. Gratitude is always the most appreciated and sprightly thing that a person can ever hear. If you are running a company, you can show some gratitude to your employees by saying thanks to them for their services. It can be your first step to build a healthy relationship with your team. When the employees feel appreciated, they will be more motivated, and they are more likely to do your job in an efficient and brilliant manner. You should be ready to see considerable improvement in the time they give to your work and the level of quality they used to deliver. Similarly, you can thank your customers for buying your goods or services. The word 'thanks' will make them feel respected, productive, happy and engaged. People take enough rejections in a single day. Amidst this, a 'thanks' from you will be nothing less than a blessing for them. When you say thanks to people, they start appreciation, and the next step after appreciation is respect.

Words Not to Use

The English language contains over a million words in total. Setting aside profane words and slang, you can use all of them in your speech. Still, there are some words that you must avoid in order to successfully influence people. Let's break them down below.

The first word is 'should' which you should avoid to use in your speech. Should reveals certain weaknesses in your personality such as a weak decision making power and an absence of commitment. If you want to show the world that you are a committed person, you cannot use the word 'should.' By not using I mean you should use it where it is crucial to use, and not in any random sentence or phrase.

Another most frequent word that we speak is hope. Hope this happens. Hope that happens. Hope I become a billionaire. If we see the word in an independent position, it has a positive meaning but when we use it in different sentences, it may suggest indecisiveness, desperation and frustration. It may suggest that something is not happening despite your continuous effort. It conveys a sense of indecision. You can replace the word with desire, ambition and goal.

Probing Questions

There are lots of types of probes that you can use. They depend on what you are saying and what you want to discover. Here is a rundown different probing questions. Some probing questions are asked for a clarification.

Sometimes a speaker speaks vaguely or in an extremely unclear language that needs clarification. See the following questions.

- What did you mean by that?

- What would you be doing in the coming week?

- Would you mind telling me something about this product?

Sometimes a speaker has concluded a session or is taking time to breathe for a while, and you are confused whether to walk away or to wait for them to start speaking for their second session.

- Is there anything you want to explain?

- Is that all?

- Have we reached the end of the session?

Zeigarnik Effect

If you have been a student or are a student, you can tell that your experience of revising exams might explain that concentration has the power to help you better remember certain pieces of information. Students get involved in cramming lots of knowledge and rigorous sessions of physical exercise. They will also be ready for taking a mock test before sitting in the real exam.

Up till now interruption during our work or study was considered as a bane for our work or study, but now studies have found that interruption can improve our focus and also our memory of the lesson that we were reading while we were interrupted. It was first discovered by a Lithuanian based scientist whose name was Bluma Zeigarnik. He experimented on the effect of observation and how does it get affected by certain changes and conditions of our brain. He conducted a study by which he found out that the faster a task stands completed, the least we will remember it. They linked forgetting of something to its completion in the brain. Incomplete tasks tend to stay in our brain for a longer time because our brain keeps reminding us that something is incomplete and demands our attention. For example, we remember what books we have to read and what notes we have to consult until we are done with the examination. (The Zeigarnik Effect Explained, n.d)

Zeigarnik did a number of experiment on different participants and later on found that the participants, who were interrupted during task, showed a 90% improvement in recalling things. The result suggests that when we desire a task to be finishes soon, we will remember it until we have completed it. Until we actively rehearse it, we will definitely forget it over time. (The Zeigarnik Effect Explained, n.d)

Pattern Interrupt

A pattern interrupt is used to switch the other person's strategy. All of us have patterns of behavior that have been made of the sequences of our habits. Habits affect us as an individual and also as a leader. All people have some kind of habit that they want to change. We have to do lot of things on a daily basis and these lots of jobs are done smoothly because we practice them each day. These automated habits that are an important part of our brain out of subconscious mind and the muscle memory. These habits rule over our lives. These tasks include driving a bike, drinking water, wearing clothes and combing your hair. The memory of the place where you sit to watch the television, the location of the remote control of the television. All these are automated habits. They are quite economical for us because we things start happening automatically, and they don't stress our thinking power that tends to free our mind of the burden of many things. When the brain is less engaged, it makes fast and efficient decisions.

Yes Ladder

If you take a closer look at people, you will know that each of them has created a predictable pattern to follow. If you understand them, you can use them to boost up sales revenues. This principle suggests that we have to be consistent when it comes to our attitudes and actions. The Yes ladder is considered as a top persuasion method that is aimed at getting the customer to say yes to the question that you have crafted for them. They can also say yes to a specific situation such as making a sales pitch or organizing a meeting with the customer. The process demands that you create a series of questions that would start in a trivial way but lose their triviality as you keep on asking more questions. Each of the subsequent question that they answer is likely to make them comply with the last one. That's how it goes on.

Studies say that it doesn't matter if the questions you are asking are relevant to the sales or not. Let's see how a salesman can create a Yes ladder.

Salesman: What is the name of this street?

Customer: This is Harley Street 113.

Salesman: Is it Woofer Town?

Customer: Yes, you are in Woofer Town.

Salesman: Great! Do you live in this glamorous house?

Customer: Yes, it is my house. Thanks for the compliment.

Salesman: Great! I just wanted to let you know that we are going to give away free estimates for house painting in the area. Can you find some time to come over to the Town Hall late in the afternoon or anytime tomorrow.

Customer: I'll be there tomorrow.

This is how the salesman can build the yes ladder. We have got a couple of yeses before making them agree on the real issue that is to make them willing for a free estimation of how much painting the house will cost. Let's break down the yes ladder into steps.

The first step is to identify what is going to be the big yes in your communication which in my case has been getting the agreement of the customer on a free estimate for a full house paint. It can be anything else such as sale of a car, sale of full house, sale of cleaning services or pest control services or any other thing.

The next step is building the ladder. Once you have noted down the big yes, you can then take a backward approach and initiate building the further rungs of your yes ladder. In the example, the salesman built the yes ladder by inquiring about the name of the street and the name of the town. Then he went on to get the fourth consecutive yes from the customer on getting a free estimate on how much painting his house would cost. This is a kind of building a yes compliance.

The easiest way to get the first yes to ask a random question that you already know. You have to identify something that you know the answer to. For example, our salesman asked the customer about the name of the street on which he was standing, then he inquired about the name of the town. He was sure that he would get two clear yeses by these questions. This proved to be a lubricant for the engine of our yes ladder. The important point to mention here is that you have to preplan your yes ladder, which mean that you should create questions that would get you the yeses you are looking forward to.

The last step is a bit risky as well. Each question will help you climb up the ladder and get close to your sales objective. You need to keep pushing a little more when you are climbing your way up. Before you go on to take the big risk, you need to exhaust at least three to five attempts. (Greene, 2017)

Hypnotic Language Patterns & Embedded Commands

English language is a very deep language and it has welcomed lots of revisions, grammars and words from other languages. We can structure the thoughts and put together a strong hypnotic language patterns. This may surprise many people that all of us at one time or another use hypnotic language in our day-to-day meet ups. It affects our lives and what also what we hear, see and feel, but sometimes we use it in the wrong way and bring out negative results. In this section I am going to discuss certain hypnotic language patterns you can use for fun, to boost up sales, for direct hypnosis and for seduction. Once you are on your way to understanding the structure, you can create your own pattern of hypnotic language and use it in your speech.

Hypnotic Pacing Statements

If you want to get the brains of the people feeling slippery, you should use some pacing statements. They should be true. Let's take a look at some of the statements.

And just breathe in....

As you hear what I say...

Just listen to what I am saying to you...

Get relaxed in that chair beside the stove...

If you closely observe, all these phrases and sentences have the power to touch the soul of the listener. They immediately grab the attention of the listener.

Subtle Hypnotic Language

Subtle language is considered as a powerful language. Let's see an example of a lawyer who is trying to convince the judge on the innocence of his client. Let's take a look at the following two examples and decide which one is more influential than the other.

I suggest to you that Mr. Adam is innocent.

Respected sir and the members of jury, you listened to the statement of Mr. Adam and examined the evidence. You may take the option that he is innocent in light of the evidence.

Now think which one of the above statements has greater influence than the other one? In the first sentence, the lawyer made a stubborn and lifeless assertion that Mr. Adam was innocent that fell on deaf ears. In the second example, the lawyer tried to recreate the images of Mr. Adam while he made the statement in his defense and also of the evidence that attempted to prove his innocence. The lawyer went into the details to explain his viewpoint to the jury, which helped him make an impact on the minds of the panel.

How to Master Hypnotic Language

Hypnotic language is something that is pretty difficult to master. It is nothing less than a passion to follow. People find themselves behaving as a silly person, but sounding silly is not the only hurdle in their learning process. People know the words and sentences but still they find it hard to practice in front of other people because they feel reluctant to do that. Some of them get nervous while others find it reluctant to utter the words that they are not used to speak otherwise.

The foremost technique to learning hypnotic language is to write it down and practice. Do this every other day and you will find it to be fun and a faster way to learning new skills. Like all the other things, daily practice helps polish hypnotic language. Divide your sessions in short periods with short breaks so that you may not get bored of the work. Feel no pressure and no effort at all. Instead do it in a fun way. Imagine that you are learning a new skill that is going to immensely aid you in your practical life. You need to jot down all the major hypnotic language patterns and then combine them by giving them short time to learn. See the following example.

"And the more you remember the relaxation that's within... that's right... this is just for you... now sit here... I am beginning to wonder... deep inside...from the core of the heart...... the depths of comfort... are yours to explore... so much more of the best of who you've always been... at heart...So much to say..." (Tyrrell, 2014)

Everybody Lives in a Different Reality

Quantum physics says that every one of us sees the truth in a different way, because every one of us creates what they see in their surroundings. The theory suggests that reality is not something that is carved in stone, and it is a pretty complex idea to fully grasp. Quantum physicists as well as meta-physicists have started to explore the idea more deeply than before. Everyone we meet has his own platform that gives them something to stand on. It is just like a moral standpoint that they have belief in. Their beliefs represent who they are and who they want to be as a person.

Some people believe that human race has been degenerating at a fast pace while others believe that if human race is doing pretty well. There is a massive shift in their perspectives. Some people think bumblebees might be the reason behind the food crisis that we are facing today in the world. Another person is of the belief that the problem of bumblebees takes the back seat and it is corruption that is a major issue for the world. This is proof that people are not seeing the same reality. They are living with different versions of reality.

Body Language For Influence

The way most people carry themselves can either help them in their affairs or hinder their progress. Human beings consistently give off signals from bodies all the time, which tells others how to respond to them. It also tells about their mood and character as well. The foremost of all is your smile. It is a robust to connect with the other people. Big smiles help people consider you as a confident and approachable person. People who wear a big smile are considered as warm, approachable and confident. A smile is considered as the gateway to building a strong relationship. People are always willing to help you and listen to you if they like your viewpoint. When you meet someone, it is quite important to wear a smile to look genuine. If you are not in a good mood, it is a good idea to recall a happy memory and produce a genuine smile. If a person you are talking to is not in a good mood, you can gradually develop a smile and win his heart.

When a person has a perfectly good rapport with you, it is quite easy to make them listen to your speech or your point of view. You should match your body movements with theirs. Mimic their movements and it will greatly help you feel involved. For example, when the person pick up a pen, you should pick up one too. If they put their hands on the table, you should do the same. That's how you will be able to secure a place in their hearts.

Conclusion

If I say to my girlfriend, "I like your dress" in a way that I am staring at the sky or my eyes are chasing a couple of rabbits going down the hole, she will be perturbed by the manner in which I said those words. Instead if I wear a smile on my face and make a direct eye contact, she will love it and take it as a compliment. Rolling of eyes, shaking of the head and other such gestures make us feel sarcastic and critical.

If you tend to look directly at the other person whom you are talking to, it will greatly help you communicate your sincerity and also add the flavor of directness to your communication. On the other hand if you look down or away most of the time, you show them lack of confidence. Too much stare at a person will make him feel very much uncomfortable and he will consider it invasive, to say the least, but this doesn't mean that you should break the eye contact. Keep in mind that you need to be relaxed and also keep it steady. Don't look away as it is going to make them uncomfortable.

Our body posture also matters a lot when it comes to influencing others. Solid research has proved that our standing positions, sitting positions and walking postures greatly affect how we make an impact on others. An active and solid posture while someone talks to you is the way to make a mark on the other people. If you are not active and have adopted a passive stance, the other person will be at an advantage. He will have an upper edge during the communication or any business deal you are going to strike.

Gestures are a part of your expression of certain emotions. They tend to accentuate your message to the people. They add emphasis, warmth as well as openness to your style. Gesturing is considered as a cultural behavior. If your gestures are relaxed and carry meaning, they will inject depth or infuse power to your conversation. Another thing that has a great impact on how you influence others is the distance you keep when you are talking to others. If you are sitting or standing closely to a person, it means that you are very intimate to them with respect to the relationship. Here moderation is the key to success. If you come too close to the other people, you may be on your way to offend them, and they will immediately become defensive. This factor depends on different cultures. In the eastern culture, there is a limit of distance between two people while in the western culture, there is no such limit. It also depends on the mood of the other person. In some cases when you get close to the other person, she may consider it a request to cut down the distance and be intimate with you.

The book has educated you how you can be a better influencer for people. It explained what methods you can use to make other people attracted toward you. It depends on different things such as how you have made your first impression and what elements have you chosen for effective communication. You have learnt the key to influence other people. You have learnt several techniques such as reciprocity, pre-giving technique, consistency and many others. You have also learned what social validation is and how social-proof works.

Influencing is about how you carry yourselves and how your portray yourselves. For example, you should express it what you say by your words. Only then there will be sufficient substance in your message. Have you ever seen someone who is speaking loudly and wearing a smile on his face? The combination is hardly a reality. When we are angry, it is expressed from our words and on the face. You should bring yourself in a certain state of mind and then see how your face looks in the mirror. From there you can calculate what expression should be paired up with what kind of words. Now you can think about something and then match your facial expression with it. This book has equipped you with the techniques and methods you need to be a highly influential person.

PART-II

The Art of Small Talk

How to Master the Unwritten Code of Social Skills, Improve Your Charisma, and Little-Known Hacks to Connect with Anyone Effortlessly

By

Jason Miller

Introduction

At some point in our lives, we have all been that socially awkward person. And whether you have come to label yourself as an introvert, or you are an extrovert who is struggling to connect with that inner social butterfly, we have to come to that place where we realize that social interaction with our peers is essential for human growth.

That said, many of us find it difficult to interact with humans. There are a lot of explanations for this, but this time around, I encourage you to stop giving in to those explanations and instead take a stand today to become better at conversations. It is going to be a scary journey, especially for those of us who are shy and reclusive, but that doesn't have to define you going forward. In this book, you can learn how to take charge of your social life and find ways to build relationships that will not only empower and sustain you, but they will nourish you in ways that you didn't think was possible.

Approach this book with an open mind. Let go of any preconceived notions you have about why you are the way you are. As I said earlier, you may have come to put a label over yourself, and what this does is to help you cope better with the distance you have with the people in your life. However, as humans, we are biologically programmed to seek out each other. There is a longing on the inside of you. Something that wants you to reach out and connect. This is perfectly normal. In this book, I share with you my journey to becoming an extrovert. Now, I use the label 'extrovert,' not because I am the typical definition of someone who enjoys being in crowds. I am reflecting on how I left the place where it was difficult for me to even establish eye contact to this point where I can meet a complete stranger, smile and start a conversation. These are milestones that I crossed, and while it was hard at first, I can tell you that over time, it got easier.

If you are planning on becoming a public speaker, this will provide the foundation or premise for that journey. In this book, you will also learn how to interact with people in a public setting because public speaking is more than just standing on stage and talking to the crowd. You have to connect with them, and while it is a lot easier to connect with people when you are in a one-on-one setting, it is not impossible to replicate that effect in a group setting. And that is just one of the many things you are going to learn in this book. So, as you flip to the next chapter, take a deep and positive breath, let go of your fears, and what you think you can or cannot do. Make your mind a blank slate because here on out, we are writing new experiences in your social life and we are going to do it in style.

So, turn over and let us begin.

Chapter One: Why is it Hard for You to Talk to People?

Before we start reeling out a three-point solution to the problem at hand, it is important to get to the root of the problem first of all. And to get to the root, we seek to answer the questions of why we are the way we are. The better understanding you have about why you act the way you do, the more effective you become at implementing the solutions. More than that, knowing the root of the problem gives you deeper insight into your personality and helps you make sense of the world around you.

Why is it Scary to Talk to People?

If we are going to look into all the reasons explaining why talking to some people might seem like a scary experiment, we will be here until 12 Sundays from now, and we still would not have exhausted half of those reasons. To save us from that stress, I will focus on just one reason. And that reason is very simple; we project our perception of ourselves on other people. Let me explain that.

When we try to talk to people (and by 'we' here, I am talking about us shy folks), we think of how they would react towards us. Before we meet people, we have a certain image of ourselves when it comes to how we look and how we sound. And often, we feel that these perceptions do not match up to the required social standards. And so every time we meet new people, we feel that they are judging us based on these opinions we have about ourselves. In other words, we think for people when we come across them. And then, on top of that, we insert our negative opinions about ourselves into those thoughts that we are thinking on behalf of those people.

Do you realize how ridiculous that sounds? But that is essentially what we do, and because we think that people are thinking these things about us, it makes it difficult to approach them. These thoughts are not always self-conceived. As in, we do not just sit down and create those thoughts. More often than not, these are things that have happened based on experience. Probably in our childhood, we had a social setting where we were embarrassed by our peers who brutally capitalized on our insecurities. Or perhaps, our parents may have directly or indirectly sowed the seeds of self-doubt in our hearts and we grew up with this unpleasant notion about ourselves.

Another possible root for the negative opinions we have about ourselves could be from the kinds of content that we feed our minds. There are a lot of books, magazines and content out there in the world telling us how we should look. And when we are different from these things, we develop insecurities about those differences. Our fear of talking to people comes from a place of insecurity and to get over it; we would first need to get over ourselves.

Where Does Fear Come From?

Fear is a biological response to anything that threatens your being. When you are afraid, the fear that you experience triggers a survival instinct bent on preserving you. So, if your fear is activated when you get into a social setting, essentially, your mind or brain is trying to preserve you from any perceived dangers in your environment, and this happens because your brain has come to look at social settings as a place that threatens your well-being. This is not something you were born with. It is something that is emphasized over time, like a habit.

Fear is not the horrible monster we have come to know. We may not be like how it makes us feel, but if you look at fear from an objective perspective and get an understanding of it, you would realize that you can harness it for your own good.

Fear keeps you alert. Now, when you indulge in fear for too long, you become paranoid. However, if you are able to plug yourself into the root of your fear, you can use that knowledge to empower yourself and what do I mean by this?

Since we now know that fear in social settings is triggered because your mind has been conditioned to think that you are being threatened every time you get into a social situation, you can now work out a process of reprogramming your mind to think the opposite. This is not something that is going to happen overnight, as it would require deliberate effort on your part. However, with the commitment, you can make it happen.

I should point out here that for a small group of us, the fear that we experience when we get into social situations is part of our biological makeup and I cannot fully go into the details of that here. This because it is something that will require collaboration with your doctor if you fall under that spectrum. That said, there are still tips you can pick up from this book along the way. I believe that biological makeup or not, there is a psychological angle to this and that is what we want to tackle in this book.

Mental Barriers to Talking to People

Have you ever been in a situation where you finally walk up the courage to talk to a person only to find yourself paralyzed completely on the spot? Even after you spent days to rehearse your lines and conversations, the moment it gets to that point where you were supposed to step onto the plate, you lose it and have that deer caught in the light situation. It is not pleasant. I can tell you for sure because I have been in that boat and there are a lot of reasons for it. Most of which have to do with fear, but seeing as we have already talked about fear in the previous segment, let us look at other reasons that explain the embarrassing situation.

1. Insecurities

We touched on this area earlier when we first started out this chapter. And we are discussing this here because this is a major contributory factor to the mental barriers we experience in our attempts at social interaction. When we try to initiate conversations with people, we are often focused on who we think we are. To make matters worse, we have negative opinions about who we are and this acts as a block in our ability to talk with people.

2. Assertion of Assumptions

When we meet a person, based on certain poor analysis like how the person dresses, the way they talk and so on, we judge them. And based on this judgement, we react. What we have done here is basically to assert an assumption that we have about the person. This causes conflict in conversations because we are unable to get past this mental opinion that we have generated about this person. There is a common phrase that says," do not judge a book by its cover." Many of us take a look at the external attributes of a person without really looking inward to know a person. And without that insight, it is going to be impossible to have a genuine conversation with said person.

3. Language

Language is one of the most complex aspects of human communication. And here, I am looking beyond the differences in our mother and focusing on our perception of what is said and being said to us. Words connote different meanings to each of us and for this reason, we develop different reactions to certain words and phrases. This would explain why certain phases that may have caused a certain group of people to laugh might cause another person to cry. These differences in language can make it difficult for us to talk to people, especially when you consider the fact that shy people are typically very sensitive.

Now that we have set up a premise for why we find it difficult to talk to people, the next course of action is to look into the fears that we face every time we get into a social setting and explore effective ways to overcome it.

Chapter Two: The Foundation of Social Anxiety and Learning to Cope

Social anxiety happens when a person develops a fear of being rejected, judged or negatively evaluated and this feeling of fear is usually brought on or triggered by being in a social setting. The manifestation of social anxiety is usually in one's performance, so in a roundabout way, you can say that social anxiety is performance issues triggered by fear from being in a social setting. If any of this sounds like something you can relate with, you are not alone. Millions of people all over the world suffer from some form of social anxiety or the other. In the next few segments, we will explore the topic in detail and come up with tips on how to maintain high performance even when you are under social pressure due to anxiety.

How to Overcome Social Anxiety

The impact that social anxiety has on our lives is tremendous. However, it does not mean that it cannot be overcome. There are measures you can put in place to help you with the daily steps needed to overcome social anxiety and a lot of these steps are things that you can start doing from your home. That said, it is important to know what spectrum you fall under when it comes to diagnosing a social anxiety disorder. It is a well-known fact that people who suffer from severe and extreme cases would need to rely on drugs and therapy to overcome their struggles. Outside that, these next few steps that I am going to talk about are things that are basically doable from where you are right. If you have already spoken to your doctor, go ahead and put the steps to practice. Build on it and through it; you can build your esteem enough to help you overcome social anxiety.

1. Confront the situation that triggers your anxiety head-on

It is human to want to immediately take yourself outside situations that cause you to feel a certain kind of way about yourself. However, if you are serious about overcoming anxiety, it is important that you put yourself out there. Just ensure that you do this in moderate and controlled doses. Don't plan on going from being a couch buddy to a cliff jumping adventurer in minutes.

2. Keep a journal

An emotional journal is there to help you keep track of your feelings. That way, you can narrow down the specific emotions that trigger your anxiety. It could be fear, anger or sometimes it could just be activities that take you down memory lane to a negative experience that you had in the past. Knowing your triggers will help you become better prepared

3. Get physical

Physical exercise has a way of making us feel good and better about our bodies, not to mention the fact that it helps you explore your mental headspace and gets you into a positive mindset faster.

4. Let go of any illusions you have about being perfect

Most people who suffer from social anxiety disorder have a problem with performance in public. And that is because they think that people expect them to be perfect. It is impossible to be perfect. Let go of the desire to get people to see you as perfect. It is okay to be you the way you are.

5. Stay positive

Being positive is an essential part of your journey to overcoming social anxiety. Train yourself to stop wandering to the dark and negative recesses of your mind. Focus instead on those things that make you feel good about you as a person and the life that you live.

Advantages of Learning Techniques and Education on Social Skills

Essentially, social skills help to prep you for easy integration into social settings that you are not familiar with. It could be for business purposes or a simple education on how to do certain things when you are in public with people. These things that I am talking about are basically what people consider as proper social skills and it can range from basic conversation to traditionally acceptable interaction based on a specific geography. It is important to learn the skills so that you do not end up offending people.

Beyond that, being knowledgeable of common social skills makes it easier to communicate, as certain social faux pas that may be regarded as disrespectful can quickly earn you the tag of rude or difficult to associate with. And when you have these kinds of tags in social settings, you might as well be wearing the scarlet letter on your forehead. People tend to avoid those that are wearing such tags.

In life, you never know how far you are going to go. You cannot always judge your progression in life based on the people you are associating with you right now. It is possible that in the course of your business or career progression, you could find yourself in some of the most amazing cities and places in the world. Beyond the language barrier which could prevent communication, there are also other things that make interaction in these kinds of settings, and having good knowledge of the social skills tell are peculiar to that region can help you understand what is acceptable and proper.

The Case for Learning About Confidence and Social Skills Together

Knowing the importance of social skills is one thing. Implementing them is another and this is where confidence comes in. A person who is confident in their ability and personality does not let that get in the way of them using the knowledge that they have gained to their advantage. Whether they are in the boardrooms negotiating the next big deal or they are pitching their brands and ideas to potential investors ... or perhaps it's a child speaking up for the first time. Whatever category you fall under, confidence is the key to executing the social skills you have gained in real life.

One way you can go about boosting your confidence is by getting rid of the notion that you are not good enough. I had a counselor who used to tell me that, "if you don't love yourself, how can you expect other people to love you in the same way." It is important to build self-care routines as well as indulge in treats every now and then to help you climb out of that hole of insecurities and self-doubt. You need to begin to take on activities that affirm the many skills that you have to reveal the true personality within and discover people who share the same interests with you. In the next chapter, we will go into more detail about confidence and how to build it. This segment is meant to set a premise for confidence and how it plays out and social interaction.

The combination of being confident and having an understanding of how people interact in a certain setting has a way of portraying us as the ideal person that people should relate with. When people have this kind of perception about you, your social life will experience a massive boost and in my opinion, this is a win-win situation for everyone involved.

Chapter Three: Building Confidence for Better Social Interaction

Confidence, as we have discussed previously, is an essential ingredient for any social interaction; whether you are talking to one single person or a group of three, the right amount of confidence can set the tone for that relationship. You may have heard people use the term "doormats." This usually refers to people who are unable to assert themselves in their relationships and this inability finds its root cause is a lack of confidence. Without confidence, you will not be able to express yourself articulately. And when you are unable to express yourself articulately, people who you are in a relationship with tend to overlook your needs. So, it is important to build one's confidence.

Where Does Confidence Come From?

To put it in very short and simple terms, confidence comes from your own perception of yourself and abilities. In other words, the image or concept you have about yourself is what feeds your confidence. If you have a very poor opinion of yourself, there is a very strong possibility that you will not be a confident person. Confidence has been linked to self-esteem issues and that explains why people with poor self-esteem tend to have poor confidence.

However, while confidence is an innate ability, I would say that the society around you can influence the level of confidence that you have. So if you have people or are surrounded by people who constantly affirm your negative opinion of yourself, this would reduce your self-esteem and in doing so, reduce your confidence. The opposite happens when you surround yourself with people who affirm the positive opinion that you have about yourself. Your confidence level will soar and you find yourself doing amazing things.

Now, some people find it easier to develop confidence. You would find children who are born confident and then you have kids who find it difficult even to maintain eye contact with their peers. Over time, the society that grooms them (which includes their family, their friends, their network at school and outside the school and so on) can determine how far the confidence level of this child goes. That said, if you are struggling with confidence, the first step to building it recognizes that you are more than the opinion that you have about yourself.

The Basic Foundation for Growing the Confidence You Need

The most common tip you get when it comes to building your confidence would be to 'fake it until you make it.' Now, this can come in handy in certain situations. However, it is important to understand that there is a fine line between confidence and arrogance. And if you are faking it, your confidence can sometimes come off as arrogance. Genuine confidence has very little to do with pride or looking down on other people. As I established earlier, confidence is all about who you feel you are on the inside and not about the people on the outside.

If you are constantly putting yourself up against the people in your environment and using that as a yardstick to measure yourself with, you have crossed the line of being confident and entered into arrogance territory. That said, here are some tips on how to grow your confidence;

1. Avoid negative places and people

Nothing pulls your confidence down faster than surrounding yourself with people who are constantly negative. Take yourself out of that environment and find a space that will nurture you positively.

2. Do not accept other people's negative opinion of you

People's notions about you may have been fed by some error or mistake you made in the past but that does not essentially define you. If they insist on identifying you with that negative trait or history, that is their problem. You, on the other hand, do not need to deal with their inability to move past that point.

3. Find your voice

For me, I think that this is the most critical part of developing your confidence. You need to find what is important to you and learn how to voice those needs. You may not have to put it into words right away, but acknowledging to yourself the things that are important to you is a great start.

4. Have a strong support system

Whether it is your family, mentor, or basically people who you often get a positive vibe off, it is important that you build your own village or community of cheerleaders. These are people who genuinely care about your well-being and see the potential that you have on the inside.

Asserting Your Confidence in Social Situations

Before going further in this book, I would like you to ask yourself the following questions; what does confidence look like for you in a social situation? Are you one of those people who feel that talking down or ensuring that your voice is the loudest makes you the most confident? If so, it is time to change that mentality. Confidence is more than just how you appear, although, that also plays a role. However, I feel that appearance and confidence basically stem from being comfortable in outfits that you wear.

A lot of people tend to focus on what they wear (in terms of the designer brand), as well as social status. They also tend to lean on their wealthy background or rich educational history like a confidence crutch of some sort. All this is well and good, but they don't necessarily help your standing when it comes to confidence in a social setting. They may open doors for you, but they will certainly not keep you in the room. Confidence in the social setting is basically learning to speak and while speaking is an essential part of expressing your confidence, listening is just as important. When you feel to listen to people, communication automatically shuts down.

It is for this reason that I firmly believe that in social settings, confidence is a juggling act between speaking and listening at the right and opportune time. Confidence in communication also extends beyond the verbal aspect. You can use your body language to communicate and confidence can be expressed in your body language. For instance, slouching your shoulders is considered a sign of poor confidence. Also, one's inability to maintain eye contact can be interpreted as poor confidence. And here is my final tip. When next you are given a handshake, ensure that the handshake is firm. That is a nonverbal display of confidence. These tiny attributes are the things that make up what confidence looks like in social interactions.

Chapter Four: Understanding the Mechanics of Human Interaction

Humans are biologically programmed to seek out each other's company. No matter how much of a loner you claim to be, at the end of the day, there is an unspoken need and desire to connect with other people. This desire is the foundation of human interaction. However, there are laws and rules that guide this process. These laws are not what you find in the constitution. What you should expect to find is the fact that there are socially acceptable behaviors that come to play when you are looking at human interaction. Beyond social skills and etiquette, this chapter was going to go in-depth on how this process works and you get some tips on playing this knowledge to your advantage.

The Basic Psychological Principles of Human Interaction

This segment is meant to focus on why we interact with each other as humans. By understanding the purpose of human interaction and the psychology that guides that process, we better equip ourselves with the right tools (or mindset if you prefer) that will get us to where we want socially.

The very first basic psychological principle of human interaction is the fact that every social relationship that we have serves a goal. Now, that goal may have been plotted out consciously and deliberately. Or sometimes, it is just something that we gravitate to naturally because it suits a need. In a situation where social interaction is deliberate, the person who makes a conscious effort to interact with specific people does it usually to meet a transactional need. For instance, the person may feel that by interacting with this particular individual, they may be able to get the opportunities that would lead to their growth in a work environment or their social status.

This is not to say that the person does it with malicious intent. This person simply sees social interaction as a means to an end. Now let us look at the flip side to this. On an unconscious level, you have this person who gravitates towards a person socially to meet some form of emotional need. This is very common with us, especially if we grew up lacking a parental figure or what we term as an ideal role model in our lives. We try to fill up that hole in our lives with the people that we meet and the relationships that we build with them. When we meet someone who we feel matches the profile of our expectations, we use the relationship that we have with them to replace our losses.

Going forward, it is important to understand why you are entering into relationships with people. And while you are on the subject, try to figure out why these people that you meet might be trying to establish relationships with you. Is it for emotional reasons or transactional reasons? The goal does not necessarily have to determine your acceptance of that relationship. It simply helps you understand where you stand with that person and how to proceed in terms of communication and all of the other topics we have addressed in the previous chapters.

Difference in Manipulation Vs Influence Based on True Connection, Intimacy and Serving Others

Given everything we have talked about so far, it is understandable if you start using the words, influence, and manipulations interchangeably. However, these words have two very distinct meanings and their application in relationships have the ability to break or build that relationship. It is therefore important to understand the differences between these two words. Because, if you take everything that you learn in this book and decide to use it to your advantage without really understanding the concept behind it, you would find that rather than building good and healthy relationships you have set the tone for manipulations and nobody likes to be manipulated.

Manipulations may yield you the results that you want temporarily, but it could go on to destroy whatever future that relationship had. Influence or the other hand, can impact the choices and decisions that the other person in the relationship with you makes. But, if you are coming from a place of genuine connection and intimacy, it has the ability to enhance communication and promote room for healthy growth. Manipulations involve the use of sinister and devious practices to get your way such practices could include lying, blackmail and threats masked as requests. Other forms of manipulations involve degrading a person to a point where they start to question their own opinions as well as the manipulation of elements in the environment to simulate control.

Influence, on the other hand, employs techniques such as concession, which is basically what happens during negotiation. It also uses authority so people in a position of authority can influence the people that they are leading. Another key principle of influence that a lot of us use is the simple act of 'likeness'. If you like a person, there is a very big possibility that you would go the extra mile for that person and a lot of us use this to our advantage. In this situation, the lines between manipulation and Influence might become blurred, but it tilts more towards influence because your emotions towards that person influence your decisions.

Basic Ideas of What People Think in a Conversation and Social Interactions

If you have ever sat down during a conversation and thought to yourself, "what is this person thinking?", you are not alone. Beyond the subject matter of the conversation that we have with people, there is this innate curiosity that makes us wonder what our conversation mates are thinking. While it is impossible to decode those thoughts at the moment (given the fact that we have no mind reader), there are certain things that can clue us into the mindset of the person. I am not going to go into the specifics when it comes to the thoughts because, different strokes for different folks, as they say. However, I am going to go into some of the different things that can influence the thoughts of a person in social settings.

The Environment

The setting where you find yourself in plays a major role in what the person might be thinking about. For instance, if you are in a work environment, the line of thought would have to relate to the performance issues or anxieties about the performance issues. That is not to say that people in these environments do not think about anything outside the place of work. But this is in line with what is generally acceptable.

The Roles that They Play

The roles that people play influences what they think about in conversations or social interactions. For instance or parents would think more in the lines of things that affect the ability to parent as well as what impacts the future of their wards or children. So, if you find yourself in a conversation with a parent to enhance the conversation, you may want to find common ground by looking at their roles as parents. It is common knowledge that many parents are very proud of their children and the moment you strike up a conversation about their kids, it is always difficult to get them to stop (just kidding).

Their Emotional State

Around Valentine's season, cakes, cards, and flower vendors experience a spike in sales and when you look into their customer base, you find out that a lot of people who buy their products are couples or people who are intending to go into relationships. This speaks to the emotional state of people during that season. My point is, when striking up conversations with people, if you decode their emotional state accurately, you may be able to key into their thoughts and establish a connection with them. During Valentine, this is what these vendors tap into to make their sales pitch.

Chapter Five: The Art of Small Talk

I think the biggest mistake a lot of people make is to assume that small talk is basically those pointless words that you use in an attempt to keep the conversation going. They failed to realize that small talk is the actual engine that drives a conversation. It may feel awkward initially, especially if you are not in an informal relationship with that person. However, if you do it right regardless of whatever phase that relationship is in, you can build a foundation that leads to death if it is what you desire. Whatever your relationship goals are, the fact remains that with small talk you can set the tone for the direction in the area of communication.

The Goal of Small Talk in Conversations

There are several reasons people use small talk in conversations and I will be going into some of them. However, just as I said in the introduction, small talk is a very important engine that is useful in driving a conversation. That said, let us look at the goals of small talk and perhaps, this will help you understand just how important it is.

1. It establishes a connection
Small talk typically evolves around relatable topics and with those kinds of topics, you can use it to get a feel of how

the person you are communicating with sees the world without really getting in-depth. This is particularly useful if you are not familiar with the person in the first place. With small talk, you can get to know the person without making an awkward situation even more awkward.

2. It is a coping mechanism for people with anxiety
Social anxiety is more common than you think and we know that it happens when you find yourself in a social setting. If you are trying to break out of your shell and get into that place where communicating with people is no longer tedious, one of the first things you would have to learn how to do is small talk. Small talk is an excellent defense mechanism as it helps you participate in the conversation without dreading the outcome of it and this is because the conversation you are having is in shallow waters, so to speak and offers you safety.

3. It opens up a window for dialogue
This comes in very handy if you are at a networking event and you are trying to get to know people. Rather than coming outright and blurting out your credentials without really getting to know the person, inserting a little small talk into the conversation can set the premise for how the rest of your

communication with that person will turn out. If you are able to do the small talk right, the person you are having a conversation with would be more open to hearing the rest of what you actually intend to say.

These three that I have just listed here are particularly useful for the objective that we have in terms of mastering the art of communication. The small talk goes beyond having to discuss the weather and in a few short moments, you are going to learn more on the subject. Just bear in mind that regardless of your personality type, small talk is essential for conversations to thrive.

Conversation Flow

If I wanted to give this topic a definition, I would say that conversation flow essentially is the smooth transition from one topic to another. When you are having an extensive conversation with a person, if you stay on one topic for too long, it might get boring. And if the topic is a sensational one, tempers might flare-up. So, it is important that you consciously apply effort in ensuring that the conversation moves freely from one topic to another. Now, in a bid to stir up the conversation flow, it is also important that you don't just jump from one topic to another. Because then, you start to look like you are unsure of what you are doing. In this segment, I am going to guide you on how to establish a healthy conversation flow even with a stranger.

Step one: Create a doorway for the conversation

A doorway is the starting point for any conversation. Whether you are in an informal setting or any place where everyone is professional, you need a doorway to get you into a conversation. Now informal settings, a lot of people tend to go with the introduction route. They start a conversation by introducing themselves. That works too, but the most effective way to get the attention of a person you want to talk to in a formal setting is to bring the focus on them. What do I mean by that? Say you are aware of what the person does for a living, you can latch onto that as the introduction. An example of being, "Hi, I overheard that you are a software engineer. Do you work primarily with websites or applications?".

A question like that will force them to respond but there's also a great chance that they would respond happily because this is a subject that they are interested in. On the other hand, if you find yourself in an informal setting, a great way to stir up a conversation is by asking questions. However, ensure that the question you are asking is not a 'yes or no' kind of question. It should be a question that will cause them to be involved in their response. An example would be, "Hi there, I am very new at all this and you look like someone who is very much at home here. So, I was wondering if you could make a recommendation for me". Again this puts the person at the forefront of the conversation. If you ask politely and keep your demeanor pleasant, you might be able to start up a conversation.

The choice of the way for the conversation should be dependent on the situation you find yourself in. If you are on a date or an interview, or perhaps you are meeting up with investors, the doorway for the conversation must match the situation.

Step two: Initiate small talk

This is the part that some people have trouble with. But if you pay attention closely, I would say that this is the easiest part. The main ingredient for initiating good small talk is listening. Now, if you end up with a person who is not really into conversations, you may have to do more of the talking, but listen to their responses as well because their responses will cue you in on what the next topic of conversation should be. For example, if you meet the person in a museum and you were able to create a doorway for conversation, rather than ask them about when they developed their passion for art, focus on the little details that they offer you. For instance, if they mention the name of a particular artist, let that be a conversation lead. Make a comparison with the artist that they mentioned with another artist and get their opinions on it.

This is small talk, but in a way, it is helping you get to know the person. So, create the doorway then listen to their responses. Pick up on topics that you are knowledgeable about and find that they are also interested in to initiate the next topic of conversation. It is also fine if you allow the other person to lead you into the next topic. Avoid being monotonous in your responses. Giving yes or no answers when you are having a small talk is a big conversation killer. So, endeavor to respond in three to four sentences and perhaps ask a few questions of your own. As you ask your questions, try not to sound as though you are interrogating the person because that makes people defensive. Instead, affirm their choices and if you don't agree with them on certain topics, politely express your view without using it as an opportunity to convert them.

Step three: Time your conversation

If you keep the conversation short and sweet, people are more likely going to remember you. However, if you continue droning on about subjects that you find fascinating, there is a very big possibility that if that same person sees you at another event, they will avoid you. Especially if they don't share the same interests with you. So, when you get into conversations with people it is important that you time it in such a way that you are able to exit the conversation when the excitement is still high. There is a proverb that says, "leave when the applause is at its loudest." This applies to conversations as well. In a bid to keep your conversation short, I do not encourage you to be checking your time because of that in its own way as rude. However, there are body signs given by your partner in conversation that you can use to decide if it is time to exit that conversation.

For example, if you start noticing that the person you are talking to is glancing about the room, that is a sign that they are looking for someone else to talk to. At this point in time, this is your cue to step back. Another important cue to look out for is if they are checking their own time. These subtle body languages are informing you that the conversation has come to an end. However, if you find that the conversation is riveting with both of you being reluctant to end it, I would still say that for a first meeting, especially if you are in a formal setting where the goal is networking, you should try to end the conversation. That said when you end the conversation with someone like this, ensure that you take their contact details as this could lead to more conversations or communications in the future. But as of the moment, your focus in this setting is to network and you want to mingle and meet up with as many people as possible.

If you are going to stick to time, then I will say in a formal setting, 5 minutes is a lot to spend with one person. That should not mean you end the conversation abruptly. You listen to what they have to say, express your fascination with their ideas and then inform them that you were pleased to meet them; however, it is time for you to move on. Exchange cards where possible and exit the conversation politely.

5 Principles For Success In Conversations

Given everything we have learned so far from the art of small talk to ensure that you have a smooth and healthy conversation flow, this segment is going to break down the guiding principles of a successful conversation. This will go on to help you identify those elements that make the conversation interesting, relatable and most importantly guarantees a repeat;

1. You are good with descriptions

In the mouth of a good conversationalist, words are like the paintbrush in the hand of a painter. The words that you use help to paint a mental picture and that picture is what your conversation partner would identify with. Your inability to use words to describe or articulate your thoughts is the reason why people have miscommunications. Because the words paint a different picture from the message that is being passed across. This is something that you are going to have to learn and groom yourself in.

2. Creative use of contrasts and comparisons

When having conversations, the comparisons and contrasts that you use have a way of enriching the image that you create. For example, instead of just saying that the beauty (of a person or thing you are describing) is delicate, you go on to say the beauty of that person is as delicate as a rose flower. What you have done there is to make the picture you are painting richer and all the more interesting. Comparisons that you use enhances the richness of a conversation.

3. The use of body language

The use of body language in a conversation is essential for the success of that conversation. Whether you like it or not, subconsciously, you are sending out messages with your body. Now, if you make a deliberate effort to ensure that the gestures you make and the facial expressions that you have matches the tempo of your conversation, you sound more interesting. And the reason for that is, your body language animates the conversation.

4. Voice inflection

Excitement can be infectious and the reason for this has been linked to the way we express our excitement. Apart from our non-verbal communication, which includes body language and facial expression, there is also our voice inflection. Have you noticed that when you are excited, your voice pitch takes on a different note? The ability to control your voice inflection is the reason why a lot of radio personalities able to drive interesting conversations over the radio even though you are not actively involved in that communication. When your voice pitch takes on a single monotonous pattern, you become bored quickly. That kind of speech pattern is best reserved for bedtime routines for children as it has the ability to induce sleep. During conversations, you want to keep it interesting so, learn to fluctuate in your voice pitch. Just remember that when you go too high, you sound crazy and when you get too low, you sound weird. Keep your pitch range somewhere in the middle.

5. *Interesting topics*

When you are having conversations with people, the topic focus should not just be a subject that you find interesting. Your partner in the conversation has to find that topic interesting too. That way, both your interests intersect. You may be one of those people who can talk about the incubation period of the caterpillar and find it so fascinating. However, not everybody is interested in the sordid details surrounding this phenomenon. So, as I mentioned in the previous segment, pick up cues as to what both of you find interesting and elaborate on that. If you apply all of the four previously mentioned principles of a successful conversation, it is bound to make the topic even more engaging.

Having laid out these five basic principles, I feel like I should point out here that no conversation can truly become successful if you fail to listen to your conversation partner. The cues for your conversation guide will come from the details obtained when you listen to that person. You may enjoy the sound of your voice and you may have some interesting contributions to make to that conversation; however, you must remember that conversation is not entirely about you and therefore, you need to give room for the other person to share their thoughts and opinions.

Chapter Six: How to Initiate Non-Verbal Communication

Before you open your mouth to speak, there are ways that your body can communicate. The information that you put out there with your body even though it is subconscious could go a long way in helping other people around you form an opinion about you. For instance, if you are in a public space and you are standing with your arms crossed across your chest, people immediately get the way that you do not want to have a conversation. And even though this is not your intention, your body language is saying you are a no-go area. So, this chapter is about helping you learn how to be more deliberate in the way you communicate without saying a word.

How to Smile

A smile is an involuntary response to something that makes you happy or brings you joy. There are a lot of scientific studies that have been conducted on the benefits of a smile and the results of these studies have linked smiles with longevity, health as well as attractiveness. It is said that smiling makes you more physically attractive and not just to yourself but to the people around you. Now, this attraction is not just about physical beauty. What this means here is that a smile can act as a social magnet that attracts people to you. When you smile in a public space, essentially, you are speaking non-verbally and telling the people around you that you are approachable and available for a conversation.

I did say that as well as an involuntary response; however, it doesn't mean that you can only smile when you feel happy or see something that gives you joy. You can deliberately initiate a smile even though you are not experiencing any of these emotions I mentioned. When I was younger, my mother was very fond of saying this, "fake it until you make it," and she was talking about my smile. I wasn't much of the smiler and anytime we went out, she was constantly encouraging me to smile. At first, when I curve my lips upwards in an attempt to smile, I felt ridiculous and somewhat embarrassed. But I found that as the seconds progressed, I genuinely started feeling like I needed to smile. Going by my experience, of course, in that first stage, the smile can seem painful. If you have ever witnessed a painful smile, you know what I mean… that one where your teeth are grinding against each other and the muscles on the side of your face become strained from the effort you are putting into a smile. That, in my opinion, is not a smile. It is a grimace.

The key to faking a smile is keeping it as natural as possible. And since we already know that a smile is an involuntary reaction to something that gives you joy, we start by focusing on elements around you that make you happy. It could be the color used in the decoration; it could be the snacks that were served, or you could focus on people that you actually like. If the atmosphere around you does not appeal to you in any way, then you could focus internally. Draw on images that make you smile; it could be an old joke or the thought of engaging in an activity that you enjoy. Let these pleasant memories motivate your smile. Now when you do smile, try not to display all of your dentition at once because then you look ridiculous and scary. A small but genuine smile is all it takes to get the wagon rolling.

How to use your eyes/body language

In romantic folklore, they say that the eyes are the windows to the soul. I don't know how true that is, but I do know this; if you do not channel your gaze properly, you can come across as one of many things and one of those things could be the vibe that you are an unpleasant person to be around. When you step into a new environment and you find yourself glancing around, people read you as someone who is nervous and with something to hide. If you decide to glare at people every time they look at you, the interpretation they will get is that you are a person with malicious intent. This also happens when it comes to body language. If your arms or legs are crossed, whether you are standing or sitting, it reads as though you are turning people away. The message that they get from you, essentially, is that you are not available for conversation.

Even if you are not having a one-on-one conversation with people, if you find yourself in a position where you are on a stage talking to a crowd of people, your body language can either support the words you are saying or contradict them. You can use your eyes to express interest in a person or express your disgust of their person. Your eyes can also make a person feel intimidated by your presence, or you can help that person feel as though they are welcome into your space. The language of the eyes and the body is one of the most basic forms of communication. When you were born, you did not have the gift of garb, yet somehow, your parents can read your expression and understand that you have certain feelings about certain things... even though you never expressly stated those emotions. As we grow into languages and understand how to communicate without words, our eyes and our bodies still have an essential message to pass across.

More often than not, I believe that our bodies have a way of communicating the true intent of our hearts. Even if your words are saying one thing, people are paying attention to the way your hands are moving and to the expressions on your face. I remember a hilarious incident that happened when I was much younger. My younger sister was being introduced to lime. We talked about the lime; about how sharp and bitter, the taste was. But this particular brother of mine was bragging about how he loved the taste of lime and so, my mother bought lime for him that day. He tasted it and of course, immediately, he was hit with the sharp sensations and although the words that came out from his mouth were, "I love it," we saw his facial expression and it told us everything we needed to know. His eyes were squeezed shot which basically told us that he could not stand the taste and his face was scrunched up in a way that further emphasized what the eyes were already telling us.

Our body language and our expressions during conversation may not be as intense as my brother's lime lying experiment, however, for people who pay attention to your body language, they get the true message just as clearly as we did.

How to Come Across and Credible and Confident Without Words

Even for the most social person, I would say that it is not every time they walk into a room full of people that they immediately feel confident. They are simply just better adept at masking their emotions. In this segment, we are going to focus on those non-verbal ways to communicate your confidence even before you say a single word. There are several books that focus on this subject because of the volume of information available on this. However, I am going to keep it short and simple by focusing on the basics. As you continue to practice your conversation skills, you would evolve and grow this list.

1. Dress the part
The dressing has a way of building your confidence, and when you look confident, you feel confident. If you are invited to an event, endeavor to put work towards ensuring that the clothes you wear to the event match the theme. That way, you do not stand out as the oddball. One thing I would like you to take note of here is that dressing the part does not mean you have to spend a lot of money on your clothing or wear designer gear. There are three things you need to focus on when it comes to dressing the part. One is your comfort, two is your style and then three is the fit of the outfit.

Comfort does not necessarily mean you have to wear slacks and bunny slippers. Comfort is ensuring that you are able to move around comfortably in that outfit without feeling as though your dressing is going to fall apart. It also means prioritizing what makes you feel comfortable over what is fashionable. So, a nice pair of flats may be more comfortable for you than a six-inch heel. The heels are very attractive and fashionable, but you risk falling down and injuring yourself. It is better to stick with sensible shoes. Choose a pair that are formal. The next part is your style. If you are not into high fashion drama, there is no need to get into the latest trends. Stick to what you genuinely enjoy. When it comes to style, again, all you need to keep in mind is ensuring that your personal style is in tandem with the theme for the event you are attending.

Finally, ensure that the clothes you are wearing are fitted. When clothes match your body size perfectly, it enhances your strengths and hides your flaws, making you look exceptionally beautiful or handsome, as the case may be. This goes on to provide you with confidence.

2. Maintain a good posture

Slouched shoulders, hunched back and a low-hanging chin are classic indicators of poor confidence and low self-esteem issues. So it is important that you maintain a good posture. Stand upright, keep your head held up high and avoid slouching your shoulders. The key to attaining the perfect posture is just like attaining a natural smile. You have to try to keep your posture as natural as possible so that you don't come off looking stiff. Because, if you look stiff, the message you are passing across to people who might be coming your way is that you are someone who is not fun and we both know that you are an amazing person for people to know. All you have to do is give them a chance. It starts by keeping the doors open. What do I mean? Ensure that your posture says you are welcoming, inviting and accessible.

3. Don't run away from direct contact

When you meet someone, you instinctively reach out your hand for a handshake. This is a ritual in communication that must be adhered to. When you are in a handshake, ensure that your grip is firm. However, don't make it too firm that you hurt the person. Another thing you have to try to do is to maintain eye contact. Averting your gaze when there is a contact might be interpreted as you being either shy or lacking when it comes to confidence. A confident person is able to hold another person's gaze. If you feel that it is too tedious to maintain eye contact with a person, try this simple trick I learned. Gaze at the person for 10 seconds, then look away to a distance that is no longer than 10 feet away from you for another 10 seconds before returning your gaze to the person. This way, you don't have to feel intimidated by that process. You engage the person with your eyes, take your gaze away for a few seconds and then return the focus to that person. In a more intimate setting, I would advise that you hold that gaze for longer. It builds the connection you have with that person.

Chapter Seven: Becoming a Master at Small Talk

Small talk is the engine that drives a conversation which eventually leads to building lasting relationships. If you are able to master the art of small talk, you will become an excellent conversationalist. People love to talk with someone who has something interesting to say. But more importantly, they also want to be heard. Small talk is not just about you talking.

It is about creating an atmosphere that allows for easy communication and communication can only happen if you allow the other person to have room to express their opinions. And just so you know, the subject of the small talk does not really matter as long as you are able to handle it delicately.

You could be discussing the weather and still make it such a fascinating subject that the other person involved becomes engaged. This is what it means to master small talk.

How to Start Small Talk

Knowing what we know now about small talk, here are a few pointers to help you get started;

Step one: Put your phone aside
Small talk is not the time to start showing off the make and model of your phone or trying to view the latest happening on Instagram. Social media has made it possible for us to connect with people all over the world; however, because of the numerous voices on the platform, it has made us more disconnected from our real world. I watched a movie once where this nice family was having dinner. And the whole room was quiet, not because the food was super delicious, but because everyone was on their phone. A platform where the family was supposed to connect with each other gave room for a total disconnect because of phones. So it is important that you disconnect from social media and your phone in order to connect with the person in front of you.

Step two: Ask open-ended questions
I talked about this earlier, but I didn't go into detail because I knew that we were going to run into this here. The questions that you ask will elicit a response from the person that you are talking to. If you ask simple 'yes or no' type of

questions, that is exactly what you would get. You need to learn to ask the type of questions that would require the person responding to use more than two sentences.

Step three: Be enthusiastic

Remember what I said about voice inflections earlier. When you inject excitement into your words, it automatically triggers excitement in the other person. This is because, as humans, we are empathetic by nature and one of the ways we show empathy is by mirroring the action or response of the other person in conversation. Your enthusasm can become contagious simply because the person empathizes with where you are coming from and they are now mirroring your reaction. It may feel a little fake initially, but the more you practice, the better you become at being excited about the topic of your small talk

Step four: Listen attentively

One thing I have always said in this book is that the foundation for your small talk is basically in the answers that you receive. When you ask those open-ended questions, the responses that you get are what will build the topic for the next set of questions and that is essentially how your conversation will grow. So, pay attention. Besides, you never can tell when the other person would ask a question of their own and if you weren't paying attention or listening to anything they were saying, you might end up making yourself and the person look like a fool.

Step five: Choose your small talk topics carefully

Small talk is not a time to express your political and religious views. Not only is there a very strong possibility that you might end up offending the person you are having a conversation with, but it also creates room for animosity and can make the person that you are having this conversation with feel defensive. When people are defensive, their guards are thrown up, leaving you on the outside. Safe topics for conversation include arts, sports, hobbies, professional interests and of course, my personal favorite, climate.

How To use the FORD Method For Small Talk

The last segment rounded off with the instruction to be careful about the choice of topics for your small talk. There I listed a few examples; however, the Ford method is one of the most reliable ways to decide on the preferred topic for small talk, especially if you are having a conversation with a complete stranger. The Ford method essentially focuses on the acronym FORD, and it means;

F = Family

O = Occupation

R = Recreation

D = Dreams

These are the safest topics to go for when initiating small talk with new people. One thing you should bear in mind, though, is the fact that people react differently to certain questions. This is because they all have their own personal experiences and those experiences are not always pleasant. For instance, a person who is not in very good standing with their family may not be too excited about talking on that subject. It is now left for you to take cues from what they say as well as their body language. The second you get that standoffish or defensive vibe from them, that is your cue to drop the subject. Do not proceed if you sense that the person you are trying to have a conversation with is not comfortable with the choice of topic. That will only ruin things for you and them.

How to Ask Excellent Questions

You would not believe the amount of diplomacy that is required in sustaining a healthy conversation even if you are just meeting that person for the first time. The reason for this diplomacy is that we live in a very sensitive world and people are now beginning to discover and leave their personal truths. Your opinions no longer govern the lives of other people. Now, I am not saying that it did back in the day. It's just that people were more tolerant of outside opinions. Not to mention the fact that they were very into ensuring that their lives were pleasing to those around them.

But all of that is rapidly changing and for this reason, you have to apply caution when you ask certain questions. Even if you are genuinely curious about what is going on in that person's life and you are certain that you have no ulterior motive, you need to respect the boundaries that people have put up and unless you are invited, certain doors on certain subjects will always remain shut. This segment is about helping you find a way to ask those open-ended questions that will not offend or cause the person you are asking those questions to feel insulted. See what I mean about being diplomatic? Anyways, let us get into it.

As I mentioned earlier and open-ended question is basically the kind of question that would require the person in the conversation that has been asked to respond in more than one sentence because it would require them to use their own knowledge and feelings an example of an open-ended question is, " what have you been up to today?". You see that there is no way a person can answer yes or no to that question, they would have to break down how their day went even if they may prefer to give the paraphrased version.

Typically, open-ended questions begin with any of the following words; why, what, describe and explain. The last two words on the list are not really questionnaires on their own; however, they can be used to elicit a lengthy response from the person you are conversing with. If your questions begin with a will, do, are, and so on, the response you are going to get is going to either be a yes or a no with little to no explanation.

The Power of Listening

There are several definitions of the word, listening. However, I would say that the one that most appeals to me is this one that says, "listening is the mindful act of hearing and making an attempt to comprehend what is being said by the other person." In other words, listening is not just hearing the words that being said to you. It is a choice that you have to make to understand what is being said to you. These days a lot of people feel that communication means talking and because we all have something to say, we feel that it must be said. And in our bid to ensure that what we have to say comes out, we fail to pay attention to the words that are coming out from the mouths of the people around us.

Active listening I am told is an essential communication skill. You cannot call yourself a great conversationalist if you fail in the area of listening. What that says about your person is that you are only concerned about your voice as well as the voice in your head. Every other person's opinion might as well be dust; you receive it, but you never make use of it. No matter how smooth you are when it comes to the gift of garb, if you are not a listener, you will not be able to engage your audience. Even in shows where you have comedians on stage doing their bit, despite the fact that the only person doing the talking is the comedian, he or she still listens to the audience for cues and it is those cues that help him deliver his performance exquisitely well.

We have already established that there is both verbal and nonverbal communication. For conversations to go smoothly, you have to pay attention to both what is being said and the body language you are getting from the person. In a situation where you have multiple people talking at once, there is very little possibility of the cause of the problem being resolved and that's because everyone is talking at the same time. The solution will only arise when one person decides to listen and hear the other party out. Mastering the art of small talk and knowing when to listen are two of the basic skills you need in order to become an excellent conversationalist.

Chapter Eight: Channeling Positivity into Your Conversation to Keep it Going

Before we go any further into this chapter, I want to say congratulations. You have come a long way from where we started and while we still have some ways to go, it is important to sit back and take note of the progress you have made so far. I also hope that at the end of each chapter, you give yourself social assignments to carry out so that you can experiment on the lessons you have learned. This is not the kind of book that you open and read from chapter to chapter, back to back, until the end.

I think that would be boring and at the same time, it will not help you assimilate the information that I have compressed into this book. So, in case you haven't been doing this already, at the end of each chapter (if possible at the end of each segment), close the book and carry out a physical social experiment. Create journals to record your experiences and proffer solutions with a focus on how you think you can improve in those areas you feel you fell short on. Now that we are done with that, let's get right on to the gist of this chapter.

How to Talk and Banter

On the surface level, talk and banter have the same meaning. However, when you go deeper into the definition of things, especially when it comes to conversations, there is a lot of difference. Talk is all we have been doing since we started this journey together from the first chapter. We have been looking at how to talk better, how to engage in small talk and generally just how to be better at talking with people. Banter, on the other hand, is a playful type of conversation. This is the kind of conversation you have with a person whom you are typically attracted to. Sometimes, we have playful conversations with people who are just friends, family members or even people of the same sex. However, for this segment, we are focusing on playful banter with the opposite sex because yes, that is part of communication too.

One major rule of banter conversation is ensuring that both you and the person (s) engaged in the conversation are aware of the fact that everything said in that conversation cannot be taken seriously. You need to apply the law of taking things with the proverbial pinch of salt because everything that you say in that conversation should not be given any kind of levity. The main ingredient for a successful banter conversation is a great sense of humor as well as this mutual understanding that I just talked about. You should be able to roll with the punches and dish out just as much as you are receiving. I have heard of banter conversations that took on a nasty turn and then again, that is not why we are here. We are looking at how to keep the conversation playful and sexy when dealing with the opposite sex without turning ourselves into maniacs.

Another important thing to remember is that banter is a playful exchange and the goal is to tease each other. This is where you display your wit. And as far as I am concerned, there is nothing sexier than wit and humor. In the spirit of keeping things playful and light, your body language should also reflect this. That stern and stiff body posture are not going to work. You need to loosen up a little. That is not to say that you should hunch your back and drop your chin. We talked about this earlier. You have to look confident. But in this case, you also have to look relaxed. Looking stiff and holding your breath at the same time will make you look constipated and I have never known anyone to like that. Finally, you have to learn to have fun with this. You are not writing an exam that your life depends on. You are simply bantering. Also, the only way to become good at bantering is practice. The more you engage in it, the faster you develop the ability to think on your feet.

How to Always have something interesting to Say

Chances are, you have met that one person who is just such a delight to talk to. They always have something to say that stirs up the conversation. That person is what we call a great conversationalist. The thing is, a great conversationalist is not someone who always has something to say. It goes beyond that. After all, is said and done, the best thing about a great conversationalist is the fact that they enter into conversations without any expectations. They don't even try to control the conversation; they just go with the flow. The only time you would find them actively guiding the conversation is when they feel that the topic is veering off into murky waters. Other than that, they just go with it. No matter what is being discussed, they seem to have an idea about it and have the ability to make a valuable contribution to that conversation. This could also be you and here's how to ensure that you always have something interesting to say;

1. Stay up to date on all current events

If you were thinking that the 10 o'clock news was for older people, I am hoping that after this segment, you will change that mindset. The local news basically, is information about what is going on in the world around us. You cannot be so consumed with your life that you fail to be aware of what this is going on. Your awareness of the latest happenings will form a major part of the contribution that you make in any conversation. A great conversationalist always stays updated.

2. Read a book

This book you have in your hand right now will provide a wealth of information that goes beyond just what you were hoping you will get from it when you opened the first page. This is what all books are like. They open you up to a world that you are not familiar with. They transport you to places and times. You can go back in time to visit the past or take a trip to the future. There is just so much information available in a book. Since information is essential for a good conversation, you may need to develop the habit of reading.

3. Think carefully about your answers before you respond

Unlike playful banter, where you allow the first thing that pops into your head to come out of your mouth, this time around you need to think carefully before you respond. At the same time, do not try to force yourself to sound interesting. People can see through your attempts and they would see as someone who is not genuine. In a bid to make yourself sound interesting, you might end up losing the interest of the person you are having a conversation with. Be relaxed, think your answers through and respond in a way that is respectful and befitting of the question you are trying to answer or contribution you are trying to make to that conversation.

How to Resuscitate a Dying Conversation

There are times when no matter how much effort you put into a conversation, we find that things are slowly drifting into a deep end. It is like watching a drunk man trying to walk on a straight line. He has very little control over his limbs and constantly teeters over an imaginary edge. In the same way, you are feeling powerless to stop the death of the conversation. I have been in that situation so many times that I can read the signs of the back of my palm. The banter slowly dies and then people start fidgeting and avoiding each other's gaze. Occasionally, you will hear someone cough here and there. When you see all these signs, know that that conversation is dying. However, it doesn't have to. By injecting your personality into the conversation and taking control of the wheel without necessarily trying to control what people say, you can get the conversation back on track. Here are my tips to help you do so without losing a single drop of sweat

Step one: Don't take it too personally

A lot of times, we assume responsibility for a dying conversation. We feel that it is because we don't have anything to contribute, or we have just too shy to say anything of value that people will find interesting. But this is not the case. Sometimes, people are genuinely tired and when they are tired, a conversation is the last thing on their mind. You have to respect that and don't try to carry the weight of the conversation. If you get the sense that people are tired, let it go. There will always be other times to chat. This is the one time you should accept that it is not your fault. It takes two to dialogue. As long as you tried to put in some effort and you are not getting feedback, you are good.

Step two: Put your newly developed small talk skill to work

If you have been practicing how to engage people with small talk, this is the best time to put it to work. Perhaps the weight of the previous conversation is making people feel uncomfortable. Small talk eases them out of that discomfort and can get the conversation going again. Remember, we talked about the FORD method. This will also be a good place to apply it

Step three: Ask questions and listen attentively to the response

Remember we talked about asking open-ended questions. This is also a great place to put that to work. The questions that we ask will give you more insight into the person and also give them the opportunity to talk (that is if they are interested in talking). I know that previously, I also emphasized the fact that it is the information that you get during this exchange, that will build on the next question. And this is just how you keep going and growing that conversation

Step four: Know when to call it a day

Here's the thing; at some point, you are going to have just to accept that perhaps this person or persons are not interested in having a conversation. And that is okay. It does not reflect directly on your person. We just talked about this in step one; this has to do with the other person. You can't control how they feel about the conversation or their decision to not contribute to the conversation. This is on them and if you are getting this kind of vibe, I would say it is best to check out politely.

How to Come Across as a Positive Person

People naturally gravitate towards someone that they perceive has warm and positive energy. Nobody wants to stand or talk with the bitter crow. And whether you like it or not, there are subconscious vibes that you give off that tells the state of your mind. The subconscious vibe I am talking about here goes beyond your body language. A positive person has a cheery disposition. I would like to point out here that being shy has very little to do with your disposition. I mention this because a lot of people tend to confuse the aversion that shy people have towards social settings with the aversion that a negative person has towards people.

Even if you are shy, it doesn't mean that you are automatically a negative person. A shy person essentially has trouble connecting with people in a social setting and a negative person on the other hand, also experiences trouble connecting people in social settings. But their experiences are not because of the same reasons.

For a negative person, it has more to do with the character traits and dark personality, which makes people avoid them. People don't avoid a shy person, as a matter of fact, because of the quiet nature of the shy person, a lot of people are not even aware of the shy person's presence. But I can tell you that they see a negative person clearly and make a choice to avoid them completely.

To project yourself as a positive person, you would have to do the opposite of everything that the negative person does

1. *Do not look down condescendingly on other people*
Negative people have a very condescending manner about them. It is almost as if they feel that everyone that they come in contact with is meant to serve them. A positive person, on the other hand, looks at everyone they meet as equals. It doesn't matter your gender, appearance or social status; a positive person automatically finds a way to connect with you. On the other hand, a negative person is looking for reasons to disconnect from you.

2. *Do not talk people down when you meet them*
This is a classic negative person move. It is all part of the condescending strategy. Sometimes, their talking down on people is not necessarily because they are very mean. They use it to mask their own insecurities. So, if they find that a person is making a more valuable contribution to a

conversation than they are, their strategy is to find a way to break that person's confidence. And they do this by talking down on them. A negative person does not appreciate the confidence in a person; instead, they see it as a threat or a challenge. A positive person, on the other hand, is constantly seeking to cheer you on. So, even when people falter in conversations, a positive person does not take that as a limitation or nuisance; instead, they encourage the person.

3. Do not engage any negative thoughts

If you are in a social setting, it is possible that the ambiance may not be as beautiful or as up to standard as you would like it to be. And these things could be in your head as you are ruminating on the entire situation. However, a positive person does their best to ensure that what is in their head, stays in their head. As a matter of fact, they go a step further by focusing on the details that are actually nice. That way, the thoughts invoke pleasant feelings and these pleasant feelings radiate into the aura. A negative person, on the other hand, takes delight in tearing apart the efforts of other people. And so they have no trouble thinking negative things and then even going a step further to air out their negative views regardless of who they hurt along the way.

Avoiding Excessive Negativity in Your Social Interactions

Now that you have figured out how to project yourself as a positive person, it is time to look at a scenario where you have other people projecting negativity on you. Just because you are trying to maintain a dialogue and build a relationship doesn't mean that you should have to take on their negativity as well. If you have learned anything along the way, I hope it includes the fact that emotions are contagious. Just as people can contact excitement from your own excitement, you can also catch negative emotions from the negativity of other people. Besides avoiding the concept or the idea of being around negative people, there is also the fact that negativity is an energy-draining exercise. If you have ever been near a with a negative person, you know exactly what I am talking about.

You spend resources, energy and effort trying to fight off that negative spirit and by the time you are done with them, you would feel exhausted. And the worst part is that you wouldn't have made any positive progress. So, resist the urge to be the person who changes the negativity of other people. If you find that you are already feeling emotionally drained every time you encounter a particular person, you need to start looking out for your own mental health. Now, stepping out of that situation takes courage. Especially if you are a shy person who is just learning how to connect with people. If you find out this person you have connected with has such negative energy, it is heartbreaking for starters. Secondly, it is difficult to get out of that situation because you know how much you struggled to even get into the relationship in the first place. But that is what the segment is about.

Before we get into how to avoid negative energy, let us talk about the signs that tell you, you are in a negative environment

1. Someone is getting hurt
In relationships, there will be times where we unintentionally hurt the other person. This kind of hurt is never deliberate and the moment it is brought to the attention of the person who is inflicting that hurt, immediately they feel remorseful and take steps to resolve the situation. However, in a negative environment, the goal is to hurt. Whether you are the one being hurt or you and the person you are with are collaborating to hurt other people, that is a negative situation and you need to get out of it.

2. You feel as though you are constantly fighting a battle
Relationships are never easy and that is because you have to diplomatically navigate through your needs, wants and compromises. However, if it feels as though everything in that relationship is an uphill climb, you may want to rethink that situation. Relationships are not really as hard as people say they are. Yes, you will encounter challenges the same when you encounter challenges in life, but if you are constantly fighting and feeling emotionally drained at the end of the day, you need to get out.

3. You have no sense of self-worth
Positive relationships have a way of reinforcing your strengths and helping you work on your weaknesses. If you are in a relationship or a situation where you feel that your weaknesses are constantly on display and your confidence is taking a beating on a daily basis, that relationship is very negative. It lacks the nurturing and encouragement that is abundant in positive relationships.

There are many more signs to look out for but these three are classic. So, I urge you to pay attention to. If you find yourself in that situation, it may be hard at first but you need to look out for yourself and take that bold step to get out of that situation. Now, if you are in a networking event or a social setting that has a semblance of a networking event, there is a chance that you would find negative people. Because where you have people in a gathering, you would find clusters of negative energy around the place. You need to step out of those clusters to avoid negative conversations.

This is how to recognize this kind of situation and avoid them:

1. When people are engaging in gossip or hurtful rumors, it may sound delightful to the ears. But remember, someone is getting hurt in that conversation. Even if the person being talked about is not present, you need to get yourself out of that group.

2. When a group of people seems to have nothing positive to say about the event, you can interject and let them know that you see some positive things. If they ignore the things you have highlighted and still go on to talk about their negative perspective, you should take that as your cue to leave that conversation.

3. If you find yourself in a cluster where the body language is dark and unwelcoming, this is a sign that the atmosphere there is negative. You don't even need to wait for a conversation, quietly pick up your things and move to somewhere where the ambiance is more receptive.

Chapter Nine: Using the Art of Storytelling to Drive Conversations

One of my favorite things about my childhood was the bedtime stories that my parents would read to me before I go to bed. More often than not, they prefer to go outside the books that they bought for me because I was the kind of child who got bored with monotony. So, they had to learn how to tell stories that I had never heard before and I tell you, it was the best thing ever. I think that it was because of those bedtime stories that I learned how to be a good storyteller. Even though I was very shy, for the people that I knew and connected with daily, they enjoyed it when I was telling a story.

It could be something as simple as my experience at the office. I learned how to add little embellishments and use certain words to make my story billboard worthy. In this chapter, I am going to draw from my own experiences as well as the opinions of experts to help you perfect the art of telling a good story. This will go on to help you perfect the art of keeping your conversation partners engaged. It is the art of storytelling that makes it possible for a great conversationalist to talk about the weather as though he or she were reading a transcript from one of Sidney Sheldon's novels.

Principles of a Good Storyteller

For starters, a good story is about an event and how the people in that story reacted to that event. A great storyteller has a good story to tell and so for you to become a great storyteller, you have to start with your story. So, let us explore the elements of a good story

1. It comes from an experience

The one thing you should know is that experiences don't have to be something that you went through first-hand. It could be something that you experience through another person. Perhaps it was a story that they shared with you or it was something that you witnessed. Either way, for a story to be good, you need to involve experience. The reason is that when you experience something, you are able to explore that experience with your senses; you know what you felt, or heard or even smelled

2. It should have a series of unexpected events

The twist and turns in the story are what makes it engaging and riveting to the listener. If your story is something that people have heard consistently, over time, they may get bored or not feel half as connected to the story as they would if everything you are laying out with something that was unexpected.

3. It can be embellished but not fabricated

Even the greatest storytellers and fictional writers draw on the experiences of other people to tell their stories. What they write about is not entirely fabricated. There are elements of truth in their stories. What they do however is to embellish the details and make it as unexpected as possible. For an introverted person, this stage here is going to be a very tough hill to climb. However, with some practice, you will get the hang of it.

How to Keep the Other Person Engaged and Listening

In the last segment, our focus was on the elements of a good story. In this segment, we are going to look at how to tell that story. Now, these are two different things but if you are able to bring them together in harmony, you would greatly improve your storytelling skills. So, let us begin

1. Speak in the language that they understand

Storytelling is lost on your listener if they are unable to comprehend you or the things you are saying. Language here goes beyond the commonly accepted native tongue. It is also about vocabulary. If you are talking with children, you would have to bring yourself down to their level and this would also include using words that they can understand. You cannot bring the University standard language into a preschool class and expect that they would understand what you are saying. In the same way, gauge the audience you are with and measure they are receptiveness to your language and then tone it down or up as the case may be, to suit their level of comprehension.

2. Tell your story from a relatable context

If people can't relate to the story that you are telling, there is a very strong possibility that you would lose them. Your message may be a very powerful and life-changing one but if they cannot understand how it impacts them or where they feature in it, you might lose your audience. One way to make your story relatable is to personalize it. Don't approach it with a futuristic perspective or out of body experience. Bring it down to a level where they feel as though they were a part of that story. Emphasize your personal experiences in that story. Highlight what you felt and how you felt and then tie that into the theme of the present conversation you are having.

3. Be animated in the delivery of your story

We talked about voice pitches and voice inflections earlier on and this goes on to emphasize that. When telling a story, if you use the same monotonous tone and expressionless face in your description, you will lose your audience before you get to the end of that story. Try as much as possible to be animated. Let your voice inject as much emotion as possible into the story. Think of it as a stage performance except that you are not on stage and your audience is not paying for your performance. However, the routine is the same. The main actor here is your voice and if you use your voice inflections correctly, you could create different characters in your story and the audience will connect with each of them.

All of this is something that you would have to learn and practice. Some experts recommend taking Improv classes to improve your storytelling skills. I say that is an excellent idea. Go for it if you can.

Chapter Ten: Building Quality Relationships and the Keys to Making Them Last

There is an old African adage that says, "when the handshake extends beyond the elbows, it becomes something else." From the first chapter to the 9th chapter of this book, our focus was establishing the foundation for relationships that first communication you have with people that then goes on to build lasting relationships. Now, we have gone past that proverbial handshake. We are now trying to get to the elbow. This is a different ball game altogether. You would need to learn new skills and this is apart from the ones that you are already developing. Some of it will come naturally to you and some of it will take some patience and understanding to get through it. This chapter is about walking you through that process. I intend to help you build good and healthy relationships no matter how much of an introvert you are.

Connecting with People by Finding Common Ground

Human beings are communal creatures. We are biologically programmed to find and connect with people who we have something in common with. The key to lasting relationships is ensuring that you are connecting with people that you can relate with. If you have nothing in common with this person whatsoever, it can be very difficult for that relationship to thrive. And the reason for this is because at some point it would seem as though the relationship is one-sided. When a relationship becomes one-sided, it becomes a breeding ground for resentment.

Today, the world has experienced the highest rate of divorce than it ever has in recent years. And if you look closely at the people involved and have a conversation with them, you would find that the whole relationship crumbled because of resentment. I have listened to interviews of people who were getting divorced or trying to salvage a damaged relationship, one of the recurrent themes in those conversations was the fact that they felt like they no longer had anything in common with this person. It is very important to have common grounds in a relationship and so before you even get into it, you have to ensure that both parties have something in common.

It could be a business goal if you are talking about formal relationships. Or shared values and belief systems if you are talking about informal relationships. Do not connect with people based on trivial things like their appearance or wealth. Over time, those things will fade away. The important things to look for are their character traits, their personalities, their dreams, and their ambitions. These are things that remain consistent over time. And when you get to know these things, you have to be able to see where you fit in because your fitting into their world as well as their fitting into your world establishes common ground. That way both worlds can come together without colliding. Lasting relationships are built through the merging of worlds and it starts from finding common ground.

How to Make Them Feel You Empathize

In today's world, the concept of empathy has evolved from its original meaning. Without going through the whole psychological babble, let me just put it this way; empathy is basically walking in the other person's shoes. In other words, you put yourself in that person's situation and have a second-hand experience of what they are going through. Today, a lot of people feel that empathy is about saying nice things when people are going through stuff. That is not empathy. That is being kind and showing compassion. Empathy allows you to understand a person's point of view and like I said, for you to be able to do that, you would have to walk in their shoes. In this case, it doesn't have to mean you going through exactly what they are going through. You would have to put your imagination to work. Picture the circumstances that they are going through, insert yourself in that situation and then look at things from that perspective. This will give you a unique understanding of a person's behavior, thoughts, and motives.

In relationships, we tend to focus on our needs and this is because we fail to empathize with those of our partners. When someone reacts to you or something that you did, we take it personally because we feel that it is more about us than them. While I am a strong advocate for making yourself the number one lead character in your life, I feel that if you want your relationship to thrive, you may have to get off your soapbox from time to time and view things from the other person's perspective. When you have the perspective of the other person, you are able to contribute in a more valuable way to that relationship. For example, a couple where one spouse stays at home and the other goes to work every day would have to struggle with resentment if either of the spouses does not take the time to recognize the contributions of the other. And to recognize these contributions of the other person, one person would need to picture themselves in the shoes.

If the partner that does not see how difficult it is to manage the children at home and then keep the home in order, they would fail to appreciate the homeliness that they always come to meet at the end of their workday. And this is because they are more focused on the tedious activities they had to face in the office. This also goes vice versa. For couples in the same situation who empathize with each other, you would find them carrying out activities to make the life of their partners easier. The one who comes home from work would not immediately start requesting things; instead they look for areas where they can contribute to the upkeep of the home. And the same goes for the person who was at home. They would not make demands as soon as the other person comes home. Instead, they will give them space to allow them mentally decompress. This is what it means to empathize with people.

How Listening Can Help You See and Make Connections

When you have an emotional need or concern, you are most likely going to go to a person who you feel would listen to you. This also works with people in a relationship. They tend to air their views to people they feel will sympathize and listen to them. This often comes into play when we are thinking of the male and female dynamics in relationships. Men are not really talkers or great communicators are generally speaking in one on one relationships. They are actionable in nature and tend to be more of doers. Women, on the other hand, invest a lot in communicating their emotions and feelings.

The problem arises when the man feels that every time the woman says something, he has to do something about what she has said. But in reality, more often than not, what the woman needs is someone who would listen to what she is saying and sympathize with her. Listening, in this case, is not just about keeping your mouth shut and leaving your ears open. It goes beyond that. Earlier on, when I was talking about the art of small talk, I did say that one of the things you need to learn is how to actively listen and listening in this context also applies the same way.

You have to pay attention to what the person is saying so that you can hear them and then understand where they are coming from. It also helps you to empathize with the person. If you are able to actively listen to the people you are in a relationship with, you will find that you automatically become their confident. More than that, because you paid attention to what they are saying and you are able to understand and empathize with them, you are put in a better position to proffer solutions to their problems.

Everybody loves to be in a relationship with a problem solver and so it is important that you pay attention to what is being said. In the same vein, do not enter into every conversation with the intention to fix the other person because then every time they have a conversation with you, you would find it difficult to hear them out. This is most likely because you are already playing these scenarios in your head where you are fixing things.

You are not the human equivalent of correction fluid. It is ok if you don't fix a situation. Sometimes, all you need to do is just listen. Everything starts with active listening.

How to make them feel like your family

Family is one of those relationships in life that we have absolutely no control over. You do not choose who your biological relations are. You are basically born into them. However, when you start socializing, you are making a conscious decision to choose who you relate with and sometimes those relations that you build create a bond that can be likened to that of a family. The love, respect and loyalty in that relationship are enough to cement your bond for a long time. But how the people get from the point of being strangers to that place where they feel like this person they are with is a relationship for a lifetime? The main ingredients there is you. As I said earlier, when it comes to families, you have no choice in that matter. But in this situation, you are in complete control.

Without realizing it, we have been given the power to decide how long our relationships last. And before you try to make that argument, yes, it takes two or more to build a relationship. But it also comes from a conscious decision on your part. You would still need to be the one to apply certain principles and boundaries to enable that relationship to thrive. When you put a plant in soil, it is biologically programmed to grow. However, there are things you can do to ensure that the plant experiences excellent growth so that it is able to flourish and bear fruit. This phenomenon also applies to relationships. As humans, we are biologically programmed to connect with each other, but it requires effort on your part to foster and nurture that connection into a long-lasting relationship. When someone becomes your family, you are saying to that person that they are more than their flaws and mistakes. And that they have earned your loyalty and your trust and regardless of what happens in the future, you would always be there for them. There is also the unspoken expectation that they would also accept you in the same way.

I would like to insert here that it is important to ensure that the feeling is mutual. If not, you are setting yourself up for disappointment. Expectations have killed a lot of relationships mostly because we expect things that we can't give or we give things that we don't expect from the other person. There has to be a balance. If the relationship has that mutual feeling, the progression from the level of strangers to the family will take a natural turn. In fact, you probably would not even need to utter those words out loud. It is an unspoken commitment. My advice is this, you have been given an opportunity now to choose who you call family, apply due diligence in that process and most importantly, obey the golden rule of relationships; treat people as you expect to be treated.

The Difference Between Sincere and Fake

Let me start this segment by stating it categorically that if you are faking anything in a relationship, you have laid a foundation for dishonesty. A healthy relationship thrives on sincerity and openness. If there are areas where you have to fake communication and genuine affection for that person, I hate to be the one to break the news to you, but that is not a healthy relationship. If you have ever been at the receiving end of fake sincerity, you would understand how hurtful it is. There are people who manipulate their way into relationships to achieve a certain gain. For them, it is all about their goals and not about the needs of the person that they are in a relationship with. If this is you, I would advise you to desist from that. However, to prevent a situation where you are at the other end, here is how you can spot a fake from the real.

1. It feels too good to be true

Everybody wants to live in a fairytale and a lot of times, because of this idea that we have in our heads, we ignore signs that are glaring at us and focus on those things that we want in that relationship. So, instead of seeing the warning labels, we put on our rose-tinted glasses and ride on the highs that this relationship gives to us. If you find that everything appears to be perfect in your relationship, there is something missing. As I said earlier, relationships are not as complicated as we make it out to be; however, there are bound to be challenged. If yours is free from challenges and it is looking like it is straight out of a fairy tale novel, take a long pause and reevaluate that relationship.

2. You have a sense that something is wrong

Our instincts are designed to alert us to dangers or threats in our environment. In a relationship, if you get the sense that something is wrong, even though you just can't place your finger on it, there is a very strong possibility that something is actually wrong. You can either decide to become a Nancy Drew in that relationship and do some behind the scenes detective work or step back until you are able to figure things out. Either way, something is off and that is your instinct telling you that perhaps your relationship is lacking sincerity you desire.

3. Nobody around you seems to like this person

Now, this is a big red flag. No matter how unlikable a person may be, to an extent, you would still find people who would be rooting for them. However, if you find that the people with whom you share a close relationship within your life are unable to accept this new person, there is a chance that they see something that you cannot. And a lot of times, that thing that they are seeing is the insincerity of this person's actions.

Timing a Sincere Compliment and How to Insert it into the Flow of the Conversation

Complimenting someone in the conversation is a way of affirming your appreciation of the person with whom you are conversing with. However, you have to ensure that the compliment you are giving is appropriate to the circumstance. In a formal setting, for instance, you cannot make compliments about a person's body part. Even if they are about things that are innocent like their Eyes or nose. It would make the person feel uncomfortable and an awkward silence could ensue. Your component should be about a personality trait or their contribution to their profession.

Outside that, the next thing you need to focus on is how you deliver the compliment. You want the high praise that you are offering to the person to come off as natural as possible without seeming as though you have an ulterior motive. In my experience, I believe that the best way to achieve that is to avoid lingering on the compliment for too long, especially if you are in a crowded space. If you have a one on one conversation with the person, of course, you could go on to emphasize that particular compliment. However, you should also note that if that one on one conversation is being carried out in a formal setting, it is best to avoid lingering on that compliment. Simply say what you want to say in the most sincere way devoid of offensive words and then move on.

The art of the compliment (without sucking up to the other person)

For this part, I would say your intentions matter a lot. If you intend to suck up to a person, the compliments that you offer to them will actually come off as that sucking up. Because it would lack the genuineness that is required when offering compliments. Again, you should also avoid lingering on the compliments that you give or constantly repeating them. This is only appropriate when you are in a very close, informal relationship with a person. Perhaps, your friend or your romantic partner. In that scenario, I think you need to linger on your compliments as often and as long as you can.

Another mistake that people make when it comes to paying compliments to people is that they feel if you compliment a person, you cannot find something wrong with them. That is not true. It is possible that you like a person's display of empathy; however, you may have a problem with how intense they are in those moments. And because you care about this person, you call them out on it. In healthy relationships, whether formal or informal, genuine compliments go hand-in-hand with constructive criticisms. If you find that you are unable to criticize a person even though you see glaring things that they are doing wrong, but you constantly find yourself complimenting them, it is safe to say that you are sucking up to them.

Chapter Eleven: Social Interactions in a Group Setting

Now, we have come to the moment of truth. In the previous chapters, we looked at initiating conversations with people one on one as well as inserting yourself into groups. Now, we are going to take things a step further. We are no longer looking at establishing a relationship with one person. We are looking at how you can carry a group along. And in this context, I am not just going to focus on networking in groups. I would look at you being a public speaker. I know that for an introvert, this is a giant leap, but that is how much faith I have in you. Because if I was able to go from being this shy kid to this person who is always excited to get on stage, I believe that so can you.

Group Conversation Flow

In a group conversation, three things can happen. You are either under the spotlight, which means you are the main person championing the conversation. Or you could be a spectator, which means that you are the one who listens more than you speak. Then you have the last situation, which I feel is the most ideal situation; you are sharing the spotlight with all the people in the group. To ensure that you are not lost in that group conversation, the first thing you need to do is identify what role you are playing.

Are you going to be in the spotlight? If you are under the spotlight, it means that you have to be the one leading the conversation, and by leading the conversation, it does not necessarily mean that you are the only one talking. Remember what I said about great conversationalists. They don't take control of the conversation. Somehow, they are able to immerse themselves in the conversation and still give everyone the room to express themselves. If you would rather play the role of the listener, you need to be an active listener. And that means you pay attention to what is being said. Understand what the person is saying and where they are coming from and then interject occasionally with questions based on the information you have received. Try as much as possible not to go off point

And finally, if you are in the last scenario where everyone is sharing the spotlight, the key to balancing it is to be both the listener and the person under the spotlight. You listen to people talking, get their point of view and then assert yourself in the conversation. There are people who have a tendency to want to talk you down. It is your responsibility to take control of your own voice. Not by increasing the pitch of your voice but by ensuring that you assert yourself. That way, you are making yourself heard and are actively contributing to the flow of the conversation.

How to Join an Existing Group Conversation

Unless you are aiming for drama, I will suggest that you enter the group as quietly as possible. And then before you make a speech, listen to what is being said. Hear the views and opinions of the people that are talking in that group and then based on the information that you get; you can then ask a question. Be warned, though; do not go into the conversation with your guns blazing. That spreads hostility and may make the people in that group feel a little bit resentful of you. Even though your point may be just what they need to get the conversation going, you need to take the gentle approach.

As you continue contributing to that conversation, you can take off your gloves and then get into it really deep. The reason I asked that you delay a little before asserting yourself is so that you are able to get your bearings. Understand what the conversation is about, know where most of the people in that group stand regarding the conversation and then assert yourself to make your own contribution. When you listen, you are able to understand more and when you understand more, you are less likely going to make a fool of yourself. This is after all our biggest fears when we get into conversations that involve groups of people.

Group Conversation Guidelines and Principles for Standing Out and Making a Connection

This here is where you learn the art of public speaking. I understand that right now you are not a public speaker, and you probably have no intention of becoming one. But at some point in your life, you may be called upon to address a group of at least ten people. If you start practicing and preparing yourself for that moment, when that time comes, you will find that you are able to have a conversation with your crowd easily and you would do this without fretting or panicking.

The key thing there is to apply everything you have learned so far. But instead of focusing on just one person, focus on the group in the room. The technique I usually use is to have the mindset that I am talking to one person but act as though I am communicating with the group. So, I try as much as possible to use the space that is available to me. For instance, if you are standing on an elevated podium, staying still in one spot does not really help you engage your crowd. You need to take a few steps at a time and keep your eyes on the crowd. You can choose a certain spot to concentrate your gaze on. Occasionally and from time-to-time, let your gaze go over the people in the other parts of the room.

Be as animated as possible in your conversation. Let your hand gestures be appropriate but do not standstill. And finally, put everything you have learned on the art of storytelling to good use. Be clear in whatever message you are trying to pass across. Let it have its starting point in a story and the story should be something that your audience can relate with. Also remember, language is important. Speak in a language that the crowd will understand and avoid the use of offensive words. For this last part, pretend as though your very existence is dependent on it. Because offending one person in a one on one conversation is bad enough. To do it in a group, that could spell the end of your career and affect your ability to speak in public.

And with that, we have come to the end of this book. But don't close it yet, I still have a few words to share with you.

Conclusion

Once again, I am so proud of how far you have come on this journey, and I am deeply honored that I was involved (even if it was in the tiniest way) to help you overcome your social anxiety and become a better version of yourself. Relationships are important. No matter the lies we tell ourselves because of our hurts and past experiences, we still need people around us. With this in mind, I would like you to subscribe to the knowledge that you are in control of the relationships that you develop in your life. You may not be able to control the actions that people take. However, you have a strong voice in determining the kind of people who stay in your life and those who don't.

Going forward, I want you to develop this mindset as you deal with people. Not everybody has to be your best friend and not everybody has to like you. You are important as a person and you deserve to be treated as though you are important. So, choose people who choose you. Treat people the way you want to be treated. You do not deserve anything less. We may have come to the end of this book but believe me when I say that your journey is just beginning. And if you can step outside of your comfort zone, I can guarantee you that life outside your door is going to be exciting and fun. There is nothing to be scared of.

Even when people tell you 'no,' that word carries a blessing. That 'no' is basically sparing you from the heartache of what the relationship would have been if they said 'yes.' And so, rejection is not the ultimate definition of your life. Some of the people you encounter would choose to walk away from you. That is ok, in my opinion, perfect even. Your mantra going forward should be "**choose people who choose me.**" I wish you all the best in your professional and social life. And I hope that from this book, you are able to become better at communication and for that reason, you are able to build better relationships. Please remember to pay it forward by passing the knowledge you have gained here to other people in your shoes.

From me and everyone who contributed to making this book a success, we are sending love, light and laughter to you.

References

Common Strategies: Common Persuasion Techniques. (n.d.). Retrieved from https://www.psychologistworld.com/behavior/compliance/strategies/overview

Eisenhauer, T. .(n.d). How to Use the Persuasion Principle of "Authority" at Work. Retrieved from https://axerosolutions.com/blogs/timeisenhauer/pulse/837/how-to-use-the-persuasion-principle-of-authority-at-work

Green, J. (2017). How to Prime Prospects to Sat "Yes" (and Make the Sale). Retrieved from https://www.phoneburner.com/blog/how-to-prime-prospects-to-say-yes/

Harmer, S. (n.d). 8 Ways To Stop Emotional Manipulation. Retrieved from https://www.lifehack.org/articles/lifestyle/8-ways-stop-emotional-manipulation.html

Layton, J. (n.d). How Brainwashing Works. Retrieved from https://science.howstuffworks.com/life/inside-the-mind/human-brain/brainwashing.htm

Making a Great First Impression. (n.d). Retrieved from https://www.mindtools.com/CommSkll/FirstImpressions.htm

Mobley, C. (2014). Softening the Sharps and tuning up normal. Retrieved from https://purposefulfaith.com/harsh-words/

Nicholson, J. (2018). 4 Ways to Use Scarcity to Persuade and Influence. Retrieved from https://www.psychologytoday.com/us/blog/persuasion-bias-and-choice/201812/4-ways-use-scarcity-persuade-and-influence

Reciprocity technique #1: pre-giving. (n.d). Retrieved fromhttps://gohighbrow.com/reciprocity-technique-1-pre-giving/

Stillman, J. (n.d). 10 Techniques Used by Manipulators (and How to Fight Them). Retrieved from https://www.inc.com/jessica-stillman/10-popular-techniques-used-by-manipulators-and-how-to-fight-them.html

The Zeigarnik Effect Explained. (n.d). Retrieved fromhttps://www.psychologistworld.com/memory/zeigarnik-effect-interruptions-memory

Tyrrell, M. (2014). Master Hypnotic Language Patterns in 3 Straightforward Steps. Retrieved from https://www.unk.com/blog/3-steps-to-hypnotic-language-mastery/

About the Author

Jason Miller is a bestselling author and human psychology researcher, a dedicated student of the human condition. Obsessed with self-improvement and fascinated by the power of the mind, his personal mission is to help people realize their full potential and reach higher levels of fulfillment and consciousness.

Jason writes books that focus on changing old habits, overcoming self-destructing behavior and the best strategies on how to deal with rejection. He is based in Los Angeles, California. Jason possesses a BSc in psychology and a graduate degree and has worked with many people from all walks of life.

www.ingramcontent.com/pod-product-compliance
Lightning Source LLC
Chambersburg PA
CBHW020529080526
44583CB00013B/785